1

A Message From Hedieh

WELCOME to financial model detective!

So let me ask you this:

- Are you a professional working on project finance deals?

- Are you a financial modeler who builds and reviews project finance financial models on a regular basis?

- Have you just got your MBA or degree in finance and are looking for a job in an advisory firm or investment bank?

- Are you a project finance associate hoping to get promoted to senior associate, managing director or partner?

- Do you work as part of a team of trainers and intend to provide a training course to executives and professionals on the topic of project finance, project appraisal or financial modelling?

If you answered yes to any of these questions, you're in exactly the right place.

This book is a step-by-step guide that shows you how to review typical project finance deals and helps you to develop your abilities to audit financial models and comment on someone else's finance model.

In fact, it hands you the exact tools and techniques I use when I review project finance deals and comment on the mechanics and assumptions that go into the financial models. It is the juice of my many years of experience working in the field of project appraisal.

Use this book as your guide as you go through the project finance financial model and impress your teammates with the quality of the questions that you will raise using the checklist provided here.

Stay $locked$! and in the meantime happy modelling!

Heideh.

GRATITUDE

___

___

Edward Bodmer

The one who made me realize that I know nothing and then gave me the courage to start learning from the beginning. He is a magician when it comes to Excel and a humanitarian when it comes to teaching and sharing his teaching materials. He is way ahead of his time. While most of the community were busy painting their spreadsheets, he was developing tools and methods to improve the way we conduct project appraisal. Merci Ed.

___

Neside Tas Anvaripour, Marc Mandaba and the whole Neo Themis team

To everyone at Neo Themis who enables me to be the lead financial modeller in so many existing infrastructure deals that I'm honored to be a part of, thank you for letting me serve, for being a part of your amazing team. Thank you Tas and Marc.

Glenn P. Jenkins

The master of investment appraisal and cost and benefit analysis. He walked me through applied economics and taught me how to develop an integrated framework of financial and economic analysis. He opened the door to African Development Bank for me, where I experienced an incredible continent and was exposed to fascinating deals. Thanks Glenn. You are always an inspiration to me.

Contents

Introduction

I used to love Kinder Surprise as a kid, and now opening up someone else's financial model gives me the same sensation. Unnecessarily complex models are like those gifts that require an engineering background to assemble; the overly simplified models are like the readily assembled figurine of dinosaurs that end up in the trash right away, and good financial models are like those gifts that you still keep in your secret shoe box.

Within the pages of this financial modeling manual, you will find hints and tricks on how to conduct a preliminary review of a financial model and decide as early as possible whether you want to work with the inherited model or build your own model instead.

So, let's get the investigation going now!

Season 1
Financial Model Autopsies

I recently posted a financial model checklist that I use when I am reviewing someone else's financial models. It is certainly not an exhaustive list and it should be the start of a conversation about what you should be looking for when reviewing a financial model. You can download it from www.finexmod.com. ⬇

Since this is a big topic to cover, I decided to break it down and go deeper in some of the important topics.

The first set of issues in the checklist are the **"Mechanical checks"** meaning things like color coding, format, integrity and basically an overall check on compatibility of the financial model with the best practice financial modelling standards.

■

Financial modelling sunday sermon

FINANCIAL MODELLING TEN COMMANDMENTS

I. Thou Shalt Keep It Simple

II. Thou Shalt Separate Inputs From Calculations And Results

III. Thou Shalt Not Hard-Code Inputs Within Formulas

IV. Thou Shalt Use Color Codes

V. Thou Shalt Avoid Long Formulas

VI. Thou Shalt Build In Error Checks

VII. Thou Shalt Include Sensitivity And Scenario Analysis

VIII. Thou Shalt Insert Summary Charts And Tables

IX. Thou Shalt Avoid Circular References

X. Thou Shalt Not Be Selfish

Figure 1: Ten commandments of Financial Modelling

```
So you shall keep my commandments,
and do them, to give eternal life to your financial models...
```

Figure 2

1. Thou shalt keep it simple

It is horrible to receive a comment from a user and even worse from an auditor that your model is complex and heavy. However, keep in mind that simplicity is a relative term and must be considered in connection with the level of knowledge of the recipient. For example, a standard financial model might be labeled as complex by someone who has little knowledge of Excel and financial modelling. On the other hand, the same model reviewed by a spreadsheet engineer can be considered as stupid.

2. Thou Shalt Separate Inputs From Calculations And Results

This is more like a Feng Shui exercise than financial modelling. For transparency and ease of access to model assumptions, dedicate separate worksheet or a separate place on a single model worksheet for your assumptions. Also, categories your assumptions by type.

3. Thou Shalt Not Hard-Code Inputs Within Formulas

This is like an environment issue in financial models. It's the same dilemma as why some people continue to throw their trash on the ground? Not that the input that you are hard-coding is trash but with hard-coding inside the formula, you are treating that piece of information as trash and burying it without a headstone or nameplate!

4. Thou Shalt Use Color Codes

Use a consistent color scheme to mark different types of cells and data. Again, keep it simple. You don't want to overdo it with too much colors or crazy, over-the-top formatting.

5. Thou Shalt Avoid Long Formulas

Use the Feng Shui rule of thumb of financial models "Do not write a formula longer than your thumb".

6. Thou Shalt Build In Error Checks

Everything might works perfectly fine in your base case but once you change any inputs, something might go wrong and you should be notified. Let me tell you a secret, I consider my models as my babies and the built-in checks as the baby monitor. So, once something is wrong in one part of my model, one of the checks will tell me that the baby needs attention. Check out my post and the excel spreadsheet on this topic titled "Check mate errors with Checks" in Financial modelling Handbook:

http://www.financialmodelling-handbook.com/2014/05/30/checkmate-errors-checks

7. Thou Shalt Include Sensitivity And Scenario Analysis

You need to do further modelling so that your model can start talking alternative future scenarios. Your model should be smart and should not suffice to a single worldview.

8. Thou Shalt Insert Summary Charts And Tables

The typical user should just validate and make changes to the inputs that you have clearly defined in your spreadsheet and then go to a summary sheet to see the main results. In this sheet, you can unleash your creativity and come up with dynamic and beautiful charts and tables.

9. Thou Shalt Avoid Circular References

They should have named this phenomenon "vicious cycle". That's what it does to a financial model.

10. Thou Shalt Not Be Selfish

Neglecting usability or user friendliness in a financial model is a costly mistake. A financial model should be easy to read and manipulate for users.

SEASON 1, EPISODE 2 ▶
In search for hidden things...

Transparency is one of the main building blocks of a standard financial model, so one of the first checks that you need to perform is to check for hidden things in the spreadsheet.

1. Use the Document Inspector

I use this as the first step to detect hidden sheets. Once you run the document inspector, you will see a summary of what it finds, and some of the items are the invisible objects, hidden rows and columns, and hidden worksheet. The downside of this is that it only lets you remove and not to unhide the hidden information. But the good thing about it is that it also detects the very hidden worksheets.

To open the Document Inspector, click File > Info > Check for Issues > Inspect Document

2. Unhide hidden worksheets

Once you have detected hidden sheets from the document inspector, you can unhide sheets by either.

• Going to Home>Format > Hide & Unhide or
• Right clicking on any tabs and click on Unhide.

3. Unhide a very hidden worksheet

Very hidden sheets are sheets that do not appear in tabs at the bottom of your workbook, nor do they show up in the Unhide dialog box. To unhide these sheets, follow these steps:

• Press Alt + F11 to open the Visual Basic Editor.
• In the VBAProject window, go through the list of worksheets and identify and then click on the worksheet that is very hidden.
• In the Properties window (Press F4 in VBA to view properties window), set the Visible property to -1 - xlSheetVisible.

4. Unhide Columns and Rows

(It means to unhide everything in a worksheet).

• Select the entire worksheet and select Unhide for each by either right mouse click; anywhere in the headings or by pressing Shift + F10 and selecting Unhide.

5. Unhide objects

Hidden objects should also be depicted from document inspector (step 1).
To manage objects in your worksheet, you can use the Excel tool called Selection Pane and accessible:

• From Home >Editing>Find & Select >Selection Pane
• Or by using the shortcut keyboard Alt + F10

6. Hidden names

The Document Inspector can also find hidden names in your workbook but cannot delete them. To view and eventually delete hidden names, you need to run a macro.

```
Sub ShowAllNames()

Dim n As Name

For Each n In ActiveWorkbook.Names

n.Visible = True

Next n

End Sub
```

7. Hidden Macros

While reviewing someone else's financial model, don't miss the macros. Even if they are no macro buttons in the spreadsheet, there might be some macros working behind the scenes.

Check the list of available macros by:

• Pressing Alt+F8 to open the macro dialogue box and you should be able to edit/view the codes.
• Some macros might not appear in the macro dialogue box. To check for hidden macros press Alt +F11 to open VBE and check for these:
• Private subroutine: The code simply starts with Private Sub name()
• Functions: another way to hide a macro from the macro dialogue box is to declare it as a function
• Also check for Private Subs and functions under worksheets in VBE. Some codes are written directly inside the sheet rather than as a separate module. In the right window pane of the VBE, you will find the list of worksheets availa-

ble in the workbook. Double click on each worksheet name to detect any codes.

While inspecting the financial model for hidden information, make sure to keep track of the list of hidden things you find in the spreadsheet so that you can report to your organization and eventually include them in your Q&A sheet on the financial model. You can download my suggested Q&A sheet from www.finexmod.com

However, many of these checks can be automated by using macros or tools that can check for these things but you can also use the excel document inspector tool and couple of clicks to spot hidden information in any spreadsheet.

Stay tuned for the next episode of Financial Model Detective.

SEASON 1, EPISODE 3 ▶
Looking for misplaced inputs

We've seen couple of techniques on how to detect hidden things in a spreadsheet earlier in the previous episode. Now would be a good time to focus solely on how you can detect misplaced inputs in a spreadsheet.

MISSION 1: Detect hard-coded inputs within calculation sheets

Background: For transparency and ease of access to model assumptions, the modeller should dedicate separate worksheet or a separate place on a single model worksheet for assumptions. Also, the modeller should categorise assumptions by type.

Detecting techniques: Use "Go To" function to identify hard-coded values in a spreadsheet. The F5 key gives you quick access to the "Go To" function.

Step 1: Save your file under another name

Step 2: Go to the first calculation sheet in the financial model and Press F5>click Special> select constants>check only the numbers box.

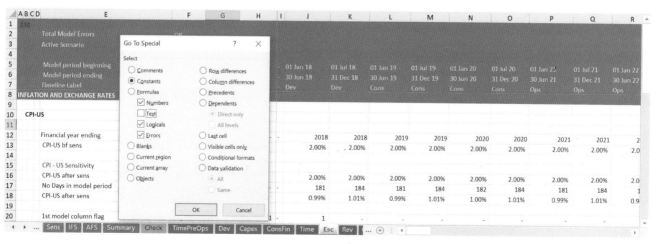

Figure 3

Step 3: Click **OK** and all constants (hard-coded inputs) will be selected.

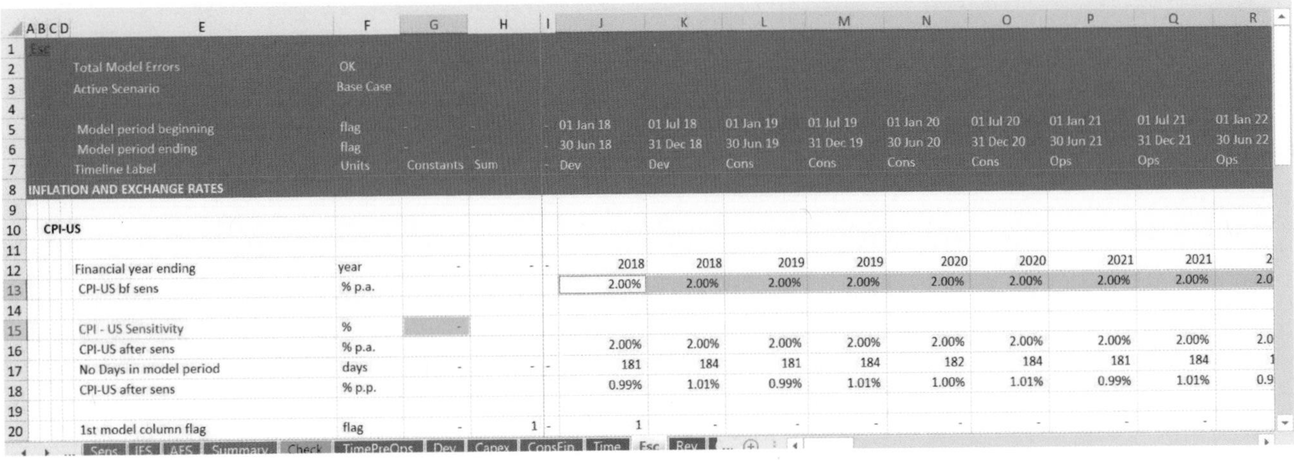

	E	F	G	H	I	J	K	L	M	N	O	P	Q	R
1	Esc													
2	Total Model Errors	OK												
3	Active Scenario	Base Case												
4														
5	Model period beginning	flag	-	-	-	01 Jan 18	01 Jul 18	01 Jan 19	01 Jul 19	01 Jan 20	01 Jul 20	01 Jan 21	01 Jul 21	01 Jan 22
6	Model period ending	flag	-	-	-	30 Jun 18	31 Dec 18	30 Jun 19	31 Dec 19	30 Jun 20	31 Dec 20	30 Jun 21	31 Dec 21	30 Jun 22
7	Timeline Label	Units	Constants	Sum	-	Dev	Dev	Cons	Cons	Cons	Cons	Ops	Ops	Ops
8	INFLATION AND EXCHANGE RATES													
9														
10	CPI-US													
11														
12	Financial year ending	year	-	-	-	2018	2018	2019	2019	2020	2020	2021	2021	2
13	CPI-US bf sens	% p.a.				2.00%	2.00%	2.00%	2.00%	2.00%	2.00%	2.00%	2.00%	2.0
14														
15	CPI - US Sensitivity	%	-											
16	CPI-US after sens	% p.a.				2.00%	2.00%	2.00%	2.00%	2.00%	2.00%	2.00%	2.00%	2.0
17	No Days in model period	days	-	-	-	181	184	181	184	182	184	181	184	1
18	CPI-US after sens	% p.p.				0.99%	1.01%	0.99%	1.01%	1.00%	1.01%	0.99%	1.01%	0.9
19														
20	1st model column flag	flag	-	1	-	1	-	-	-	-	-	-	-	

Sens | IFS | AFS | Summary | Check | TimePreOps | Dev | Capex | ConsFin | Time | Esc | Rev

Figure 4

Step 4: Once all constant are selected, open the **Format Cells** dialog by pressing **Ctrl + 1** or go to Home tab > Font> Fill Color and change the background color to red.

Step 5: You'll have to repeat the above steps for each worksheet individually.

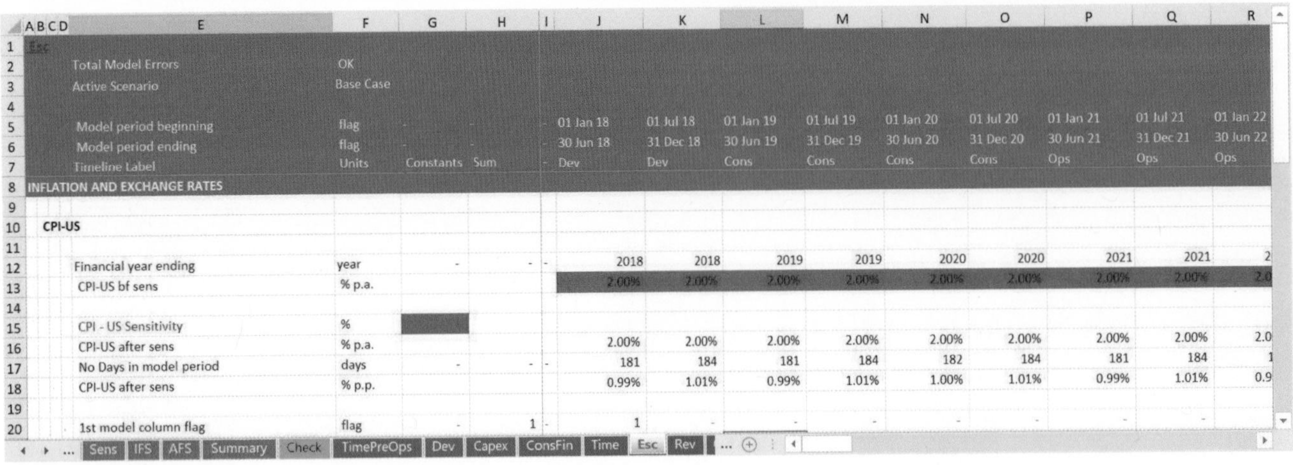

	E	F	G	H	I	J	K	L	M	N	O	P	Q	R
1	Esc													
2	Total Model Errors	OK												
3	Active Scenario	Base Case												
4														
5	Model period beginning	flag	-	-	-	01 Jan 18	01 Jul 18	01 Jan 19	01 Jul 19	01 Jan 20	01 Jul 20	01 Jan 21	01 Jul 21	01 Jan 22
6	Model period ending	flag	-	-	-	30 Jun 18	31 Dec 18	30 Jun 19	31 Dec 19	30 Jun 20	31 Dec 20	30 Jun 21	31 Dec 21	30 Jun 22
7	Timeline Label	Units	Constants	Sum	-	Dev	Dev	Cons	Cons	Cons	Cons	Ops	Ops	Ops
8	INFLATION AND EXCHANGE RATES													
9														
10	CPI-US													
11														
12	Financial year ending	year	-	-	-	2018	2018	2019	2019	2020	2020	2021	2021	2
13	CPI-US bf sens	% p.a.				2.00%	2.00%	2.00%	2.00%	2.00%	2.00%	2.00%	2.00%	2.0
14														
15	CPI - US Sensitivity	%												
16	CPI-US after sens	% p.a.				2.00%	2.00%	2.00%	2.00%	2.00%	2.00%	2.00%	2.00%	2.0
17	No Days in model period	days	-	-	-	181	184	181	184	182	184	181	184	1
18	CPI-US after sens	% p.p.				0.99%	1.01%	0.99%	1.01%	1.00%	1.01%	0.99%	1.01%	0.9
19														
20	1st model column flag	flag	-	1	-	1	-	-	-	-	-	-	-	-

Sens | IFS | AFS | Summary | Check | TimePreOps | Dev | Capex | ConsFin | Time | Esc | Rev

Figure 5

MISSION 2: Detect hard coded figures within formulas.

Background:
Best practice is to avoid hard-coding figures within formulas and to have all inputs documented in a separate section of the financial model.

Detecting techniques:
"Bird view" technique: Make cells display the formulas they contain, instead of the formula result by going to Formulas>Show Formulas. You can quickly detect hard-coded figures if there are any within formulas.

=Time!R$5	=Time!S$5	=Time!T$5
=Time!R$6	=Time!S$6	=Time!T$6
=IFS!R48	=IFS!S48	=IFS!T48
=IFS!R42	=IFS!S42	=IFS!T42
=R35 + R36	=S35 + S36	=T35 + T36
=R37	=S37	=T37
=MAX(R39, 0)	=MAX(S39, 0)	=MAX(T39, 0)
=MIN(R39, 0) * NOT(R26) * NOT(R27)	=MIN(S39, 0) * NOT(S26) * NOT(S27)	=MIN(T39, 0) * NOT(T26) * NOT(T27)
=Time!R66	=Time!S66	=Time!T66
=R40	=S40	=T40
=R32	=S32	=T32
=IF(R43, R39, R44 * R45) * 90%	=IF(S43, S39, S44 * S45) * 90%	=IF(T43, T39, T44 * T45) * 90%
=R46 * -1	=S46 * -1	=T46 * -1
=R46	=S46	=T46
=R50 *0.1	=S50 *0.1	=T50 *0.1
=R50 - R51	=S50 - S51	=T50 - T51

Figure 7

"INQUIRE": This is an "add-in" developed by Microsoft itself. You can use the spreadsheet INQUIRE to analyse your spreadsheet and get a report showing detailed information about the workbook as well as details of all formula within the workbook that contains a hard coded value.

To enable INQUIRE in Excel

Go to File > Options > Add-Ins. Manage box, select COM add-Ins and click Go.

Tick the box next to INQUIRE and click OK.

Start the workbook analysis

Click **Inquire > Workbook Analysis.**

Under items, scroll down to Formula and then select **"with numeric constants".**

In the results pane, you will now see details of all formula within the workbook that contains a numeric constant or a hard-coded value within a formula.

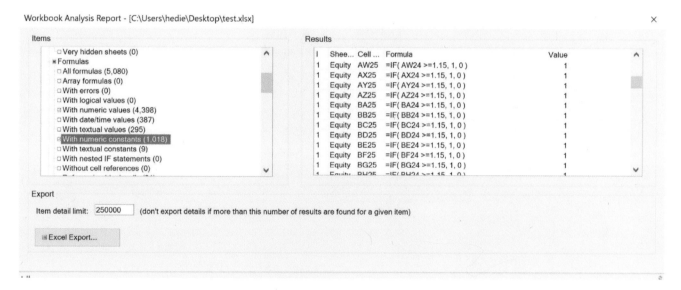

Figure 8: Screenshot of the Workbook Analysis Report

Note that if a sheet within a workbook has more than 100 million cells, you will get an error message and you will not see results directly in the results pane. You can however export the data to a report by clicking the Excel Export button.

Formulas With Numeric Constants (1,018 total)

C:\Users\hedie\Desktop\test.xlsx

Sheet Name	Cell Address	Formula	Value	Reviewer Comments
Equity	F2	=IF(Master_Integrity<>0, "Something is wrong! Ple	OK	
Equity	J17	=J42 * -1	0	
Equity	K17	=K42 * -1	0	
Equity	L17	=L42 * -1	0	
Equity	M17	=M42 * -1	0	
Equity	N17	=N42 * -1	0	
Equity	O17	=O42 * -1	0	
Equity	P17	=P42 * -1	0	
Equity	Q17	=Q42 * -1	0	
Equity	R17	=R42 * -1	0	
Equity	S17	=S42 * -1	0	
Equity	T17	=T42 * -1	0	
Equity	U17	=U42 * -1	0	
Equity	V17	=V42 * -1	0	
Equity	W17	=W42 * -1	0	
Equity	X17	=X42 * -1	0	
Equity	Y17	=Y42 * -1	0	

Numeric Formulas | Numeric Constant Formulas

Figure 9: Excel results from Inquire

Last step is to list your findings in the Q&A sheet.

High	High Impact
Medium	Medium Impact
Low	Low Impact

Matters arising from review of Financial Model Filename: "Power Project v1.xlsx "

No	Impact level	Category	Reference	Issue/Question
1		Inputs within calculation sheets	Esc, row 13, cell G15	For the purpose of transparency and ease of access to model assumptions, please transfer all of the model's hard-coded assumptions in the "Input" sheet.
2		Hard-coded figures within formulas	Equity rows 46 & 51	A number of inputs are hard-coded within formulas. Please transfer these assumption in "Inputs" where they can be easily seen and modified.

Figure 10 : Screenshot of the Q&A sheet included within Excel

Stay tuned for the next episode of Financial Model Detective.

SEASON 1, EPISODE 4 ▶
The verdict

Wrapping up the mechanical Review

In the previous episodes of Financial Model Detective, we've seen some techniques that would enable you to check if a financial model is structured, flexible and transparent.
You can use the same techniques to check for most of the issues included in the financial model review checklist.

	Check	Comments
Model Mechanics		
▶ Does the model uses a consistent colour scheme?	✖ 0	
▶ There are no errors in the model (worksheets and named ranges, macros...)?	✖ 0	
▶ There are no links to external files?	✖ 0	
▶ Are Inputs separated from Calculations and Results?	✖ 0	
▶ Uniform column structure across all worksheets?	✖ 0	
▶ The units of measurement of each element in the financial model are clearly defined?	✖ 0	
▶ Use of unique formulas across rows?	✖ 0	
▶ Model does not contain overly long and complex formulas?	✖ 0	
▶ Are there error checks?	✖ 0	
▶ There are no circularities in the model?	✖ 0	
▶ All macros included in the model run properly under base and sensitivity cases?	✖ 0	
▶ Model allows users to run sensitivity tests on key parameters like delays, cost overruns,...	✖ 0	
▶ Model include output calculations such as financial statements ratios and valuation calculations?	✖ 0	
▶ Model include a summary sheet containing key model inputs and outputs and charts?	✖ 0	
▶ There are no hidden or password protected sheets or macros?	✖ 0	

Figure 11: Screenshot of the mechanical issue list in the checklist

The verdict

After you have performed the preliminary review, you should decide as early as possible whether you want to work with the inherited model or to build your own model instead.

Here are some of the typical conclusions:

1. Model is not structured

Evidence:

• Inputs are not separated from calculations and output.
• Hard-coded parameters that are subject to change.
• Long formulas.
• Non-conformity in column structure between worksheets.
• Links to external files.
• Inconsistent formulas across rows.
• Model contains circular reference(s).
• Missing design and color-code specification.

The verdict: *For the crime of building a badly-structured model, the financial model is sentenced to restructuring.*

2. Simple tool for a complex transaction

Evidence:

• Does not meet the objective of the model.
• Does not reflect the realities of the project.
• Model cannot accommodate expected future changes.
• No programming of timelines.
• Limited number of years projected.

The verdict: *The financial model needs to be restructured to meet its objective and to reflect the realities on the ground.*

3. Black box

Evidence:

• The size of the file is too large.
• Long waiting time to run the model.
• Excessive use of IF statements (long formulae).
• Excessive use of copy-and-paste macros.
• Model contains password-protected sheets or codes.

The verdict: *The financial model is found guilty of unnecessary complexity. In the case of password-protected spreadsheets, if the password cannot be recovered then the financial model needs to be rebuilt from scratch.*

4. Model is standard and need minor adjustments

Evidence:

• Inputs are clearly defined and stated in the financial model in a structured manner.
• Model is easy to audit and understand.
• Key outputs are presented effectively.
• Model allows sensitivity and risk analysis.

The verdict: *The financial model is in line with best practice financial modelling standards and can be used during the appraisal of the project.*

NOTES:

Keep in mind that simplicity is a relative term and must be considered in connection with the level of knowledge of the recipient. For example, a standard financial model might be labeled as complex by someone who has little knowledge of Excel and financial modelling. On the other hand, the same model reviewed by a spreadsheet engineer might be considered too simplistic.

The level of details and complexity also depend on the objective of the financial model. For example, a single pager and simple but structured spreadsheet can be sufficient for the purpose of preliminary project screening.

Season 2
Financial model Soul searching

In the previous episodes of Financial Modelling Detective, we've seen some techniques that would enable you to check whether a financial model is structured, flexible and transparent. We only tackled the mechanics or physical body of the financial model and basically performed autopsies on the model. Now it is time to turn to what is important: the inputs. Pull out your flashlight magnifier and let's get into the inputs scene.

Getting into the inputs

Be up to date. If you are responsible for working and maintaining the financial model, make sure that you let your supervisors and your team know that you need to be involved and aware of all aspects of the project. Also make sure that you are involved in the missions and site visits. It makes so much difference when you see things and have a tangible vision of the project. Then when you model the different aspects of the project, you have more clarity and it also increases your sense of agency to get things done. Therefore, make sure you have this discussion with your team and give them the above arguments as to why you need to be kept up to date on all aspects of the project.

Read, read and read. Make sure you have access to the project documents and read everything you can find on the project. You might think that getting the project information memorandum will be enough for you to extract the important information, but this is not true. The PIM is mainly a marketing tool and is intended to project a rosy picture of the project. As a financial modeler, you need to read every clause of any contract, and if it is something that has financial impact, you should crosscheck whether it is included in the financial model and whether it is modelled as it is reflected in the contracts. I usually devote three to four days to just go through the documents to understand the nature of the project. In this process, I create a sheet within the model I call 'raw data' and I dump all useful information I find from the documents into that sheet and put the references there so that I can crosscheck with the model when I start reviewing the inputs.

Benchmarking. If you want to make comments on the values, you need to have reliable benchmarks. Remember that just because you are not an expert in the field, doesn't mean that you should be shy about asking questions. Ask your team if they have done comparable projects in the past and request them to share the financial model and other useful documents with you. You can also go online and try to find reliable resources. Remember that while benchmarking, you should be very careful to compare apples with apples. For example, you cannot compare the cost of a hydro dam project with a hydro run-of-the-river project and conclude that the cost of the latter is overestimated.

Question everything. When it comes to inputs, allow you question everything. You must look at the past and what has been done up to now, understand what today's project realities are and what might happen in the future. So for each input, try to find the reference in project agreements, and if it is not from the contract then try to understand the rationale behind it. If it is a price or a cost, find out where that estimate stands relative to market standards.

Different perspectives. We all see the world from different perspectives. In the field of project appraisal, different parties tend to have different points of views on the way things will evolve for the project. These are the typical stereotypes:

Lender: Lenders are mainly known to be conservative or better say more conservative than sponsors. So lenders lenses are darker and you can sometimes say that sponsors' worst case scenario can be the lenders' base case scenario. For example, in a solar power project, when the generation and eventually the revenues depend on the sun shining, the generation numbers will come from a probability distribution. Lenders will pick the conservative P90 scenario meaning that a scenario where there is only 90% chance that the number would fall less than what is expected. Or when it comes to contingency provisions, lenders will think of a scenario with higher contingency needs than what sponsor might think sufficient.

Sponsor: Sponsor thinks average and uses the estimates with 50% likelihood of occurrence as their base case estimates. I read this phrase in a great post by Oxford Global Projects saying "You want the flight attendant to be an optimist, not the pilot "; this is so relevant when it comes to financial modellers. Let your colleague who is preparing the presentation slides for selling the project to be optimist, as a financial modeller, you should be realistic and not biased.

Think base case, best case and worst case estimates. No matter if you are from lenders, sponsors or authority's side, while reviewing the financial model, always think range and spectrum. For example while reviewing the inflation rate used, first understand whether the estimated rate in the model is low, high or average and for each estimate to the extent possible, come up with these three estimates "Up, down and base". This way when you want to perform scenario analysis, you can use these estimates to come up with these 3 scenarios.

Be aware but open minded. Being a financial detective does not mean you should be unpleasant to the recipient of your comments. No matter which side of the story are you, a project finance team and its stakeholders are like a family. The aim of everyone is to get the project done but each with different incentives. So for example, if you are reviewing the model from the lenders or government side, don't assume that sponsors are thieves and they want to overestimate costs to increase their return or if you are on the sponsor side, don't make the assumption that lenders and government are against you and are over pessimistic. Just know that you should understand things and find the rationale behind every assumption. There might be a reasonable explanation for any abnormality in the assumption so just be curious but have an open mind.

In the next episode of Financial Model Detective, we're going to look at a typical project financial model as prime suspect and go through the issues that you need to look for in 'timing' assumptions.

SEASON 2, EPISODE 2 ▶
Timing

In the previous episode, we talked about general things to consider when you get to reviewing the inputs. I hope that you had that conversation with your team and that you are going for a site visit soon.

In this episode, we are going to look at a typical project financial model as the prime suspect and go through the issues that you need to look for in "Timing" assumptions.

Project finance is like a living human being with three stages of life and a financial model should reflect all stages of project's life:

Development Phase

When the baby is growing inside the womb: The preparation stages, where you get the permits, do the studies, negotiate the con-

tract. It is the idea stage and as you progress, contracts will get firmed up and different stakeholders will get involved and will eventually lead to financial close. So, the start of development stage is when the initial investors or project developers start spending their first penny on the project and it ends with when you sign the agreements and are ready to drawdown on debt and equity and pay the EPC down payment for starting the construction work.

Since the model should reflect the realities of the project, you should have these parameters in the model:

ABC D	E		F	G	H
1 InputC					
2	OK				
3 TIMING ASSUMPTIONS			Units		Comment
4					
5	Development start date		Date	01 Jan 18	
6	Time lag between start of dev. works and financial close		Months	12 Mth(s)	
7	Financial close date		Date	31 Dec 18	

Figure 12 : Timing assumptions 1

note: it might not be necessary to start with the development phase and it might be enough to start from construction. This is the case for example, when the developer is not the equity provider and will basically exit the project at closing with a premium. In this case, the historical costs incurred by this developer is of no interest to anyone and you can just take the reimbursement of development cost and the development premium paid to the developer in the project cost which is typically payable at closing.

Construction Phase

After you have recovered from celebrating the financial close, it is time for the construction works to start. It is when the baby is born and the start of headaches and sleepless nights comes up.

There is a start to construction which starts with the financial close and it ends with the finalization of the construction works.

3	TIMING ASSUMPTIONS			Units		Comment
4						
5		Development start date		Date	01 Jan 18	
6		Time lag between start of dev. works and financial close		Months	12 Mth(s)	
7		Financial close date		Date	31 Dec 18	
8						
9		Construction Start date		Date	01 Jan 19	
10		Construction Program		Months	24 Mth(s)	
11		Construction End		Date	31 Dec 20	
12		Delay in Start-up		Months	0 Mth(s)	

Figure 13: Timing assumptions 2

If you remember from the previous episode, for the sake of flexibility and transparency, the model should accommodate different sensitivity parameters on timing. So check if the model can answer these questions:

What if there is a gap between financial close and start of construction work?

What if there is a delay in construction works?

Where to look for this information?

What is the Financial close date? For an estimation of the closing date, you need to realistically look at the project calendar and understand whether the timeline provided is realistic.

Do the developers have all the required permits?

How far are the different advisors from different parties in submitting their final version of their studies?

Where are the banks in terms of their appraisal?

Are they ready to go to their board within the scheduled date?

What is the Length of construction?

Usually construction timing is from technical studies. It is the engineers who should answer how long it is going to take to build the power plant and getting it ready to be connected to the grid. If you don't have a technical study, you can look at similar projects of the same scale and come up with an estimate of the duration of the construction.

Operation Phase

This is when the project is mature enough to pay back its debt and start generating income. It starts with commercial operation date and has a specific life and ends with shut-down.

3	TIMING ASSUMPTIONS	Units		Comment
4				
5	Development start date	Date	01 Jan 18	
6	Time lag between start of dev. works and financial close	Months	12 Mth(s)	
7	Financial close date	Date	31 Dec 18	
8				
9	Construction Start date	Date	01 Jan 19	
10	Construction Program	Months	24 Mth(s)	
11	Construction End	Date	31 Dec 20	
12	Delay in Start-up	Months	0 Mth(s)	
13				
14	Operation Start	Date	01 Jan 21	
15	Duration of the concession	Yrs	20 Year(s)	
16	Operation End	Date	31 Dec 40	

Figure 14: Timing assumptions 3

Where to look for this information?

Operation start date is mainly the construction end date +1. However, you might want to add a delay in start-up sensitivity parameter to check what If the construction ends but the project cannot for some reason start producing. For example, in case of power plants, you might have the power plant ready but there might be delays in building the necessary transmission line and therefore, the plant will remain idle till the transmission line is put in place.

Duration of operation

Like human lives, this parameter is mainly project specific. If you have a sale contract like a power purchase agreement or some sort of concession agreement, then you take the duration of the sales contract as the duration of operation in your model. If you don't have a long-term contract, then you can use the economic life of the asset or to just take the life of debt and add couple of years for contingency and sensitivity. This is important because your model should cover the life of the debt. If you are considering a debt with a maximum tenor of 15 years, then your projections should at least cover 18 years of projections. If that is not the case, then you should red flag this and ask for longer projections.

Periodicity

This is about the length of each model period. Whether the projections are on monthly basis, Quarterly, Semi-annually or annu-

ally? You need to be able to justify or question this choice in the financial model. This is a project specific and also depends on where you are in the appraisal stage. However, as adjusting the model to changes in timing is a structural change, I advise you to build flexibility in model periodicity.

I usually model construction on monthly basis because it is a critical stage in project's life and you will want to monitor month by month of construction. However, when it comes to operations, you can use the periodicity of the repayment of debt as the base for choosing the periodicity during operation. For example, if the lenders require a semi-annual repayment of debt, you make your operation projection on semi-annual basis. So watch out for this in the models that you are reviewing and if you find any issues there, you better point out and get it fixed right away because changing it at later stage might require a complete restructuring of the spreadsheet.

3	TIMING ASSUMPTIONS		Units			Comment
4						
5	#Months per pre-operation period		#		1	monthly
6	#Months per operational periods		#		6	semi-annualy
7						

Figure 15 : Timing assumptions 4

Snapshot of the Timing assumptions from the preliminary financial model checklist:

	A	B	C	D	E
1	**Preliminary checks on the financial model**				
2					
3		Project Name:			
4		Financial model File name:			
5		Audit date:			
6					
7				✔ 1	For yes enter 1
8				✖ 0	For no enter 0
9					
10		0% 10% 20% 30% 40% 50% 60% 70% 80% 90% 100%		check	
11				Check	Comments
27	**Timing**				
28		Does the model contain necessary flags and counters to accommodate changes in key dates like financial close date, construction start and end date, operation start and end date?		✖ 0	
29		Does the model provide flexibility in periodicity of forecast periods both during construction and operations?		✖ 0	
30		Sufficient number of years of financial projections?		✖ 0	

Figure 16 : Snapshot of the Timing assumptions from the preliminary financial model checklist

In the next episode of financial modeling detective, we will continue our search in a typical project finance crime scene and we will look at the red flags in the construction cost assumptions.

CapEx

We've mentioned the common issues related to the key timing assumption previously. Now we will go over the capital expenditure assumptions and some of the typical issues that you need to be aware when reviewing this section of the inputs sheet.

Check with contracts

In order for you to make any comment on the cost estimates, you need to understand what each cost line item represents. First thing is to refer to project documents and see if there's any sort of construction contract and check if it matches with the estimated reflected in the model. Check for the dates and validity of contracts. For example, if a quotation is valid for 3 months and you don't expect to get anything signed within the expiry date, then check if you need to adjust the cost at closing to take the inflation into account.

Reasonable cost breakdown

In some cases, financial model does not contain any details of CapEx and have only a one-line item as CapEx including all construction expenses. This is problematic for different reasons:

• For transparency and also audit you need a reasonable breakdown of CapEx. You don't need every detail of brick works and kilos of cements, just a general cost of civil work, same for equipment and other costs.

• Tax and accounting depreciation of assets might differ based on type of assets.

• Lenders and lenders advisors will require a breakdown of costs to be reflected in the model. Keep in mind that the breakdown might not be available at an early stage. However, you should still ask the financial modeller to include a placeholder and can be left blank until later stages when the information is at hand.

Local content versus foreign content

Usually financial models fix a unit of currency and reflect all cash flow items in that specific currency. However, it is important to examine the contractual invoiced currency of each cost item. What are the arguments?

For sensitivity on foreign exchange, all costs payable in any currency other than the currency of the financial model should be reflected in the invoiced currency and converted to model currency using the forward looking foreign exchange rates.

If you are approaching development banks and agencies for financing, they will most probably require this information. They use this information in their development impact analysis

Treatment of inflation

You need to watch out for the treatment of inflation in costs. Again for each cost item, you need to ask the question, whether that cost item is subject to inflation and or is it a fixed contract and any overrun will be on the contractor. For example, the EPC might be a lump-sum contract spread over the construction phase so you don't need to apply any inflation on the EPC cost but you need to cross check that with the contract. On the other hand, other cost items like the SPV budget during construction might be subject to inflation. And here's another that I didn't mention above on the necessity of having the breakdown of CapEx in the model.

Contingency provision

If you remember from the last episode, we said project finance is like a living being and unexpected happens in different stages of everyone's life. It is the same for the project. So the best we can do to make sure that our project can move ahead with the schedule plan is to provide provisions. So there is no doubt that contingency should be budgeted in both timeline and project budget.

However, I have never come across any scientific method of coming up with the optimum amount of contingency to be added in the budget. But what I know is that the amount of contingency varies from project by project and depending on how advance the project is or at which stage of its lifecycle the project is at. For example, a hydro damn project with 5 to 6 years of construction might require 30% of total project cost as contingency on the hand a 3% to 5% might be sufficient for a solar project with 12 months construction. Also, at the early stages

when you have no clarity on the contract negotiations, you might want to include higher contingency and once the contracts are firmed up, you can reduce the contingency amounts if under the contracts, is responsible for any cost overrun.

So while making your comments on the amount of contingency take these aspects into account.

Development cost and premiums

To bring a project up to closing, the developers will need to invest money on the development phase which is the riskier stage in a project's life. That's when you hire advisors to do various studies, get your permits and approach lenders to secure funding. Throughout this process, the developer will not be remunerated for the development activities. It is only when the project closes that the developer can recap its development costs and gets a premium on it. So, having a cost item as development costs and a separate one for development premium paid to the developer is a typical cost item that needs to be included in the model. And all of these cost needs to be documented and the invoices will be audited by different advisors. These are real costs, but you can still check for the amounts and question the level of premiums.

Taxes applicable during construction

I am currently working on a project where the tax advisors failed to indicate all the taxes that the project needs to pay during construction, so we didn't budget for the taxes that the project is now paying and is eating up the entire contingency.

Again, for each cost item, ask the questions: what are the taxes applicable to this cost items? Is it included in your cost estimated?

Advisory fees

Remember from the previous episode, we said question everything. When it comes to advisory fees, try to understand who is getting this fee. Is it really a third party advisory firm hired by the SPV to deliver an expertise or is it just a management fee for the sponsors? If it is a management fees, then see if it is justifiable. It is perfectly fine if the sponsors have the expertise within their team to handle tasks that otherwise should have been handled by third party and of course they need to be remunerated for doing it. So for each cost item, when you want to question, ask respectfully and show that you are just trying to understand things and you are not objecting anything (at least not before understanding it).

CapEx payment milestones

Once you are done with your log list of questions on the CapEx, you can check the payment milestones.

For example, for EPC, you should check for the payment schedule included in the contract. If there's no contract yet, then you should assume a down payment topically between 10% to 30% and remembering you can sculpt it throughout the construction. Some other cost like SPV budget can be spread equally throughout the construction. On the other hand, some cost are payable up-front at closing like the reimbursement of development capital and development and insurance premiums.

So again, for each cost item, you need to check the payment schedule. This is important because it is going to determine the drawdown schedules on debt and equity.

Snapshot of the CapEx section from the preliminary financial model checklist:

	A	B	C	D	E
1	Preliminary checks on the financial model				
2					
3			Project Name:		
4			Financial model File name:		
5			Audit date:		
6					
7				✔ 1	For yes enter 1
8				✖ 0	For no enter 0
9					
10			0% 10% 20% 30% 40% 50% 60% 70% 80% 90% 100%	check	
11				Check	Comments
31		Capex			
32			Model reflects estimates of anticipated capex with relevant breakdown (ideally based on budget offers), including range of contingencies?	✖ 0	
33			Capex items are reflected in their original currency of invoice and converted to model currency?	✖ 0	
34			Are the capex figures adjusted for inflation? In other words, are they expressed in nominal terms?	✖ 0	
35			Benchmarking : does the total project cost estimate is in the market range?	✖ 0	
36			Is there enough contingency provision to cover unexpected financial and technical cost overruns?	✖ 0	
37			Does the model take any taxes payable during construction into consideration?	✖ 0	
38			Are payment schedules of capital costs over this construction period are in line with the contracts? Or if the contracts are not yet firmed, is there an acceptable level of pre-payment (between 15% - 30%) is included for EPC?	✖ 0	

Figure 17: the CapEx section from the preliminary financial model checklist

SEASON 2, EPISODE 4 ▶
Financing

You cannot talk about financing cost without knowing who is going to finance what. So, first thing is to look in the project documents for timesheets with different financiers:

Reference docs:

• Joint Development agreement or draft inter shareholder term sheet: You can understand how the equity is structured from these documents. For example, whether the shareholders are planning to include a shareholder loan and if yes what's the proportion of pure equity versus shareholder loan? You need to consider that there are also fiscal or accounting constraints and limits to shareholder loan amount.

• Term sheet with lenders: if there's such a document then you can get all your debt terms base on the terms reflected in the term-sheet.

Typical financing inputs to be included in the financing assumptions section of Inputs:

Gearing or debt to capital ratio

In project finance model, debt to capital ratio is mainly an input to the model and is used to size the debt. In PF deal, banks usually finance up to a maximum of 75% of total project cost. Again this is project specific and gearing might be higher or lower but it's an input and you can see this limit in the term sheet with banks.

Drawdown

Next important question, is what the priority in is drawing down for financing costs during construction. Lenders usually require the equity to put some money up front before they disburse. Or they might be fine with a pro-rata drawdown of debt and equity.

You can again find this out from the term sheet and if the negotiations didn't still get into these discussions then you make sure that the model is flexible to include different drawdown schedules.

List of financing instruments

Equity: equity can come in different forms: pure equity, shareholder loan, mezzanine debt. If such instruments are already in place for the project then you just need to crosscheck that the model reflects their correct terms and conditions. If there's no information, then you might want to have at least a shareholder loan as an option in the model in case it needs to be activated at later stage.

Debt: Again, if the debt instruments are in place then you just need to cross check with the term sheets. If not, make sure at least 2 tranches of loan are modelled.

Shareholder loan terms

Remember that shareholder loan is the most junior debt in the cash flow waterfall and any payment under shareholder loan should be treated the same as dividends meaning that any payment under shareholder loan should be subject to dividend lock up and other distribution lock ups required by lenders. However, this instrument is helping shareholders to go around the accounting constraint of limiting distribution to net profit and distribute available cash for shareholders under interest and principal on shareholder loan and also it has tax saving implications. In certain judiciary, they allow interest on shareholder loan to be deductible.

Maturity: You can have a defined tenor for the shareholder loan, but I usually model it using a %s cash sweep. So, in every payment date, a fixed %s of cash flow available to shareholder goes to the repayment of shareholder loan and the remaining will be distributed as dividends.

Interest rate on shareholder loan:
This instrument can be interest fee or can have any interest rate the shareholder requires unless there's a regulatory limit that needs to be considered.

What is important is that this interest can be deferred and normally is capitalized during construction (meaning that it is not paid and funded with debt and equity during construction, but it is included as part of the capital and carried forward to operation for reimbursement).

Repayment of shareholder loan:
As I mentioned above, the repayment of shareholder loan can be either a fixed repayment or can be based on cash sweep.

250	Equity			-	
251		Equity		-	
252			Pure equity	40.00%	%
253			Shareholder loan	60.00%	%
254				-	
261		Shareholder loan		0%	
262			Shareholder loan grace period # mnth after COD	6.00	Months
263			Shareholder loan grace period	5.00	Years
264			Shareholder loan interest capitalisation period	5.00	Years
265			Shareholder loan interest rate	11.50%	% p.a.
266			Cash Sweep %s	60.00%	%
267			Financial Closing	01-janv.-20	Date
268			Shareholder loan first interest payment date	31-déc.-24	Date
269				-	

Figure 18: Shareholder loan assumptions

Senior and subordinated debt facilities

I have included a list of typical debt terms for senior lender debt tranches here below. You need to have these inputs for each tranche of senior loan separately. Again, if there's a term sheet, then you just use them as references in your review, if not you need to come up with estimates based on similar projects. Some banks publish a catalogue of their financial product and you can get a range for some of the fees they charge.

Maturity: Dependent on the specific characteristics of the project.

Grace period: As normally, the project does not generate any revenues during construction, the project needs at least a grace period of 6 months plus duration of construction

Interest rate margin: Dependent on the specific characteristics of the project. But you might want to ask about possibilities of hedging the interest and the cost of it.

Commitment fees: Banks typically charge a commitment fee of on the undisbursed amount of their maximum committed amount and it is payable at each disbursement date.

Up-front fees: Banks typically will charge a front-end fee of up to fixed of their maximum commitment amount. This fee is generally payable not later than the date of first disbursement.

Repayment methods: Different principal repayment methods need to be modelled. Equal instalments of principal, annuities, bullet repayment and step-up or step-down amortization of the principal ...

Periodicity of debt service: It's important to understand whether interest and any other charges are payable semi-monthly, quarterly, monthly... and whether the interested banks are flexible in payment frequencies.

Currency: you need to investigate the currency of payment of each tranche and if different from the model currency, all debt flow (drawdowns, interest, fees, principal, ...) should be reflected in the denominated currency and converted to model currency using forward looking foreign exchange rates.

189	**Senior Debt 1 Terms**			
190				
191	Senior Debt 1 Timing Assumptions			
192	Senior Debt 1 maturity	#Years	15 Yr(s)	
193	Senior Debt 1 grace period: # of months after construction Period	Months	6 Mth(s)	
194	Senior Debt 1 grace period	#Months	30 Mth(s)	
195	Senior Debt 1 Drawings start date	Date	01 Jan 19	
196	Senior Debt 1 First principal payment date	Date	30 Jun 21	
197	Senior Debt 1 Last payment date	Date	31 Dec 33	
198				
199	Senior Debt 1 Interest Rate and Fees Assumptions			
200	Senior Debt 1 all-in interest rate	% p.a.	5.00%	50.00
201	Senior Debt 1 Commitment fee	% p.a.	1.00%	
202	Senior Debt 1 Front-end-fee	%	1.25%	
203	#days in the period for interest calc.	days	360.00	
204				
205	Senior Debt 1 Repayment Profile Assumptions			
206	Senior Debt 1 Principal repayment profile	Switch	2=Annuity	
207	1=Straight-line			
208	2=Annuity			
209	3=Sculpted Fix			

| ▸ ... | **InputC** | InputS | Sens | IFS | AFS | Summary | Check | TimePreOps | Dev | Capex | ConsFin |

Figure 19: Senior Debt assumptions

Debt service reserve account
In project finance deals, lenders normally required the borrower to maintain a debt service reserve in the Debt Service Reserve Account, in an amount equal to a specified number of monthly payments of principal and inter-est. This reserve account is either pre-funded as part of the project cost or can be backed up by a letter of credit.

Here are the typical inputs for the DSRA section:

234	DEBT SERVICE RESERVE ACCOUNT ASSUMPTIONS			
235				
236	**DSRA ACTIVE**			
237	Is DSRA pre-funded?	Switch	FALSE	
238				
239	**Pre-Funding of DSRA**			
240	Pre-funding of DSRA amount	Switch	1	Equal to 6 months debt service (P+I)
241	1 Equal to 6 months debt service (P+I)			
242	2 Equal to a pre-defined amount	million USD	1.00	
243				
244	**Debt Service Provision**			
245	DSRA required amount: #months of look forward debt service	Switch	6 Mth(s)	
248	LC Cost (% Target Debt Service)	% p.a.	2.00%	

‹ … | **InputC** | InputS | Sens | IFS | AFS | Summary | Check | TimePreOps | Dev | Capex | ConsFin | Ti … ⊕ ⋮ ◂

Figure 20: DSRA assumptions

Snapshot of the financing section from the preliminary financial model checklist:

		Check	Comments
Interest and financing fees during construction			
	▶ Interest payable during construction is included in the project budget?	✖ 0	
	▶ Typical fees like commitment fees, up-front fees, MLA fees are calculated and included in the financing	✖ 0	
	▶ Pre-funding of Debt Service Reserve Account is incorporated in the project budget (if required by banks	✖ 0	
Sources of Funds			
	▶ Identified sources of funds have been reflected in the model? (Senior Debt, Subordinated Debt, Mezzanine Debt, Shareholder loan, Pure equity,…)	✖ 0	
	▶ Uses of Funds = Sources of Funds	✖ 0	
Financing			
	▶ Multiple tranches of debt are modelled?	✖ 0	
	▶ Does the model provide flexibility change key debt parameters like grace period, tenor, interest rate, fees,…?	✖ 0	
	▶ Different debt repayment methods including annuity, straight-line, bullet, balloon and sculpted are built into the model?	✖ 0	
	▶ Debt tranches are fully repaid at the end of their maturity?	✖ 0	
	▶ Lock-ups on dividend distributions and other constraining factor such as accounting restrictions and lockups imposed by lenders are modelled?	✖ 0	
	▶ If required by lenders, DSRA is properly modelled?	✖ 0	

Figure 21: Snapshot of the financing section from the preliminary financial model checklist

SEASON 2, EPISODE 5 ▶
Operating and maintenance costs

Now we have almost finished everything related to construction phase and we can step into the operation horizon when the project is mature enough to stand on its own feet and pay for its own expenses. In this episode we are going to look at the Operations and Maintenance expenses.

Issues related to O&M expenses are like those we discussed in episode 3 for CapEx. So I can either copy and paste the CapEx and replaced word CapEx with Opex or I will let you rewind and check the CapEx section while having Opex in mind.

I would however like to stress on couple of issues.

Inflation and escalation

Make sure the Opex items are reflected in nominal meaning that they are adjusted for inflation. If they tell you that the model is real, then try to convince them to convert to revise and make it nominal. If they tell you that no one knows what the inflation rate will be in future, then that's the case for everything else in the model! So, make sure you understand the indexation applied and applicable to each Opex item.

Fixed versus variable Opex

We started this season saying that while reviewing or building a financial model, you should have a good feel about the project. When it comes to operation, you should understand how the operating expenses behave relative to sales activity. In other words, you should be able to differentiate between fixed cost which do not vary with production and variable costs which are functions of production. For example, for solar projects, you typically have no variable costs so it is ok to reflect all costs as fixed cost. In other instances, you need to be more careful because some cost items might have both fixed and variable component, for example fixed labour/permanent and variable labour/temporary workers.

Major maintenance costs

Major maintenance costs are typically recurring costs required after certain years of operation. For example the replacement cost of batteries or inverters in a solar project. These maintenance costs should be modelled. I have seen in many instances where the major maintenance cost is annualized as part of the Opex and is reflected in among the fixed costs. This means that project is going to set money aside for the upcoming scheduled major maintenance. However, you need to check whether there is a contractual agreement that guarantees that the money is going to be set aside in a reserve account and if that is the case then it is better to model a major maintenance reserve account rather than just annualizing the major maintenance as part of Opex.

Here are some typical inputs required to model O&M and major maintenance cost.

Snapshot of the O&M section from the preliminary financial model checklist:

142	OPEX ASSUMPTIONS		
143			
144	**Fixed O&M**		
145	O&M	USD per year	640,000
146	Insurance	USD per year	500,000
147	Project Management	USD per year	300,000
148	Administration Expenses	USD per year	150,000
149			
150	**Variable O&M**		
151	Other Opex	USD/KWh	-
152	Spare	USD/KWh	-
153	Spare	USD/KWh	-
154	Spare	USD/KWh	-
155			
156	**Contingencies and Escalation Rate applied to O&M**		
157	Escalation Rate applied to O&M	% per year	2.00%
158			
159	MAINTENANCE COST		
160			
161	Cost of heavy maintenance	US$/W	0.02
162	Cost of heavy maintenance	million USD	1.00
163	heavy maintenance reccurance after X years	Years	10.00
164			

▶ ... **InputC** | InputS | Sens | IFS | AFS | Summary | Check | TimePreOps | Dev | Cape

Figure 22: typical inputs required to model O&M and major maintenance costs.

Snapshot of the O&M section from the preliminary financial model checklist:

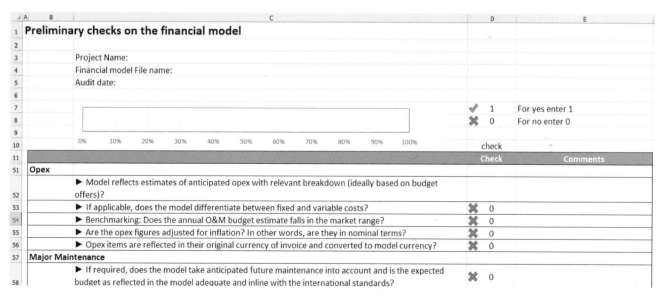

Figure 23: O&M section from the preliminary financial model checklist

Revenue

Now let's deal with the king which is the cash but don't forget that the financial model is the queen.

CASH
IS KING

FINANCIAL
MODEL IS

QUEEN

No matter what the project is all about, revenue is nothing but price multiply by quantity. So, while reviewing the revenue section of the inputs, use these hints:

Have a good understanding of final product of the project. There might some technical issues behind it and you can refer to the technical studies done for the project or if there are no studies conducted yet, you refer to studies done on similar projects.

Make a time series graph of quantities produced, price and revenue and check how they are evolving through time and question the growth rate or any escalation rate applied to revenues and its component. Again, keep an open mind and just try to understand before criticizing.

Look for the currency of invoicing and billing and check whether it has been reflected in the model. Same as for costs, revenues need to be reflected in the original invoiced currency and converted to the model currency using forward looking foreign exchange rates.

If the price is contractual, then you just need to make sure that the prices reflected in the model matches what's in the sales agreements. However, if it's the market price, you need a proper market study to give you an opinion and different set of scenarios for future prices.

There might be instances where the project generates revenues during construction. These revenues should be handled with care and here are there are different ways to include these revenues:

To be conservative and exclude them from the model and assume that these revenues will not materialize.

Include the revenues but do not use them as a source of financing and will basically be as contingency during construction and carried forward to operation phase. There is a slight chance that lenders will allow sponsor to distribute these generated cash during construction. Usually, any payment to shareholders is blocked during the senior debt grace period

.

Include revenues during construction as source of financing and reduce the debt or/and equity accordingly. However, this is risky because if these revenues do not materialise, the project will face cash shortfall and delays which is very costly for the project.

We will cover fiscal aspects in the next episode but since we are now deep into revenue assumption, we can also question taxes applicable to project revenues. Is the tariff inclusive of any tax?

Is the project charging VAT on its output? Is it included in the tariff? At what rate?

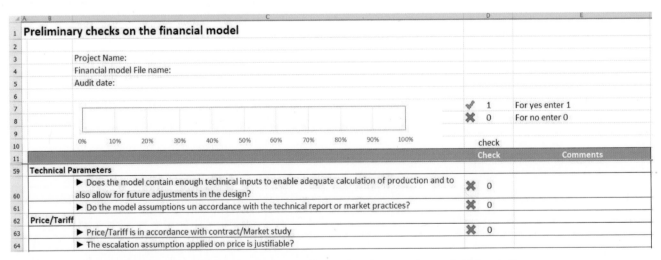

Figure 25: General queries related to revenues from the financial model check list

SEASON 2, EPISODE 7 ►
Fiscal and accounting

In the cost and revenues sections in the previous episodes, we touched upon couple of issues related to taxes on cost and revenues. Here we will expand it and cover typical tax and accounting issues you need to look into while reviewing the model.

Resources:

• Usually sponsor hires a tax advisor to draft a report on taxes applicable to the SPV. If you have this report then you can get all the information and crosscheck it with the model.

• You can also find a lot of resources online. The big 4; they mostly publish annual country by country tax guide. Just Google the " tax guide" followed by the name of the project country or where the SPV is registered and you will find reports that can help you as a starting point to understand level of taxes your project is subject to.

• Also look under World Bank Doing business. In the tax section, you can see the list of general country by country taxes.

Dig into taxes payable on costs

Make sure all taxes payable on CapEx and Opex are covered. You can create a table like the below example and ask for the party responsible to give you this information:

Table 1: Taxes payable during Development Phase

Taxes payable during Development Phase	VAT rate	Any other Taxes(%)	Any other Taxes(%)
Project identification			
Prefeasibility studies			
Design			
Structuring			
Contractual arrangements and financing			

Table 2: Taxes payable during Construction Phase

Taxes payable during Construction Phase	VAT	Any other Taxes(%)	Any other Taxes(%)
Total Development Costs			
Development fee			
Construction, including materials, equipment and labor			
Structuring			
Field supervision of construction			

Table 3: Taxes payable during Operational Phase

Taxes payable during Operational Phase	VAT rate	Any other Taxes(%)	Any other Taxes(%)
Fixed Costs (Labour & Management)			
Variable Costs (materials and maintenance)			
Insurance			

Value Added Tax

- If VAT is refunded – what is the processing time and realistic delay in receiving the refunds (both during construction and operation)?

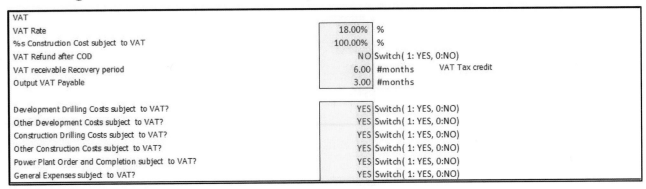

Figure 26 : VAT assumptions

Corporate Income Tax

Investigate on what should be the basis for calculation of corporate income tax and whether the tax calculation complies with relevant tax laws.

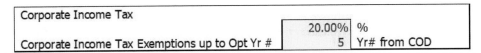

Figure 27 : Corporate income tax assumptions

Withholding Tax

Check if interest payments are subject to any tax like withholding tax? Do the same for shareholder loan and dividends.

Presentation of Financial Statements

Investigate if the financial statements as presented in the financial model are in accordance with the relevant accounting system.

Depreciation and Amortization

Look into tax and accounting life of different qualifying capital expenditure.

SEASON 2, EPISODE 8 ▶
Sensitivity parameters

Up to here, we went through the base case estimates and as we noted in the introduction to this season we said while reviewing the base case, always think *"what if…"* Now it is time to do *"what if"* analysis.

Identify risk variables

The first step is to come up with some critical project parameters which have significant impact on project results. For this you need to test the variables that you suspect having important impact using the financial model.

Understand the risk

Once you have identified couple of parameters as being important in terms of their impact on the results, then next step is to find rational explanations on why you think a certain parameter might change and to what extent. For example, if the sponsors have signed a contract with the contractor for the construction of the plant and any cost overrun beyond what is in the contract is the responsibility of the contractor and not the project then applying sensitivity to EPC will not make much sense.

Typical sensitivities

In most project documents, you see typical sensitivities like 5% to 20% deviation in CapEx, Opex, and revenues. This might be fine if we just want to have a feel of the importance of the parameter in the metrics we are monitoring. But referring to the previous point, you need to understand the risks and see its possibility.

Construction Risk

This is the risk that the construction will not be completed within the specified budget (CapEx risk) and expected timeframe (delay risk). There are a number of studies done on construction cost overrun in infrastructure projects. So cost overrun is a reality and everyone involved is trying to pass the risk to someone else. The lenders will not accept this risk and will ask for different type of completion guarantees from the sponsors. The sponsors on the other hand try to shift the construction risk on the constructor to the extent possible. For example, technical risk and any political and change in lows will be pushed to the government and there are contractual agreement and guaranteed and liquidated damages that will be put in place. So make sure you are aware of these arrangements before you apply a 50% increase in CapEx.

Opex Risk

Same thing we said for CapEx also applies to Opex. For example, in most infrastructure projects, at least for the first few years, they hire a reliable O&M contractor who guarantees the smooth operation of the project and therefore any cost overrun will be on the contractor and not the project. So you need the breakdown of Opex to evaluate the riskiness of each Opex item and apply different range of sensitivities to different cost items.

Revenue Risk

You need to consider the possibility that the project might not generate enough revenues. This might be either because of the price (price risk) or due to quantities (volume risk). You can test and do break-even analysis and check by how much volume and prices should go down to trigger default and lower the equity return to certain threshold. However, if the project is under a long term contract that guarantees that the buyer will buy a certain volume of the project's product and under a specific price (take or pay contract) then decreasing the volumes beyond a certain point might not make sense. So again make sure that you are aware of all the agreements and realities before you propose or conduct any sensitivity.

Interest rate risk

If the interest rate is floating and not fixed, the increase in interest rate can be a risk. You can perform a break-even test and see by how much the interest should go up to trigger default.

Foreign exchange risk

Remember from our CapEx, Opex and revenue discussions, we mentioned that for all cashflows, we should check for the original invoiced currency of each cashflow items and reflect it in the model using the denomination as per contract and convert to model currency. Having built this in the model, it enables us to do sensitivity test on the impact of change in foreign exchange rates.

Season 3:
Case Closed

Just to recap, in season 1, we checked the main mechanical issues related to the structure and design of a financial model.
In season two, we checked the typical issues related to the assumptions that go into the model.

Once you do the above steps, you can turn the page to outputs and check on the model results.

Sources and uses of funds statement during construction.

In this episode we are going to look at the most important statement related to the construction phase which is the sources and uses of funds statement. In season 2, episode 3 we covered the construction cost and in the following episode we looked at the financing costs and instruments. Any typical project finance model should contain a period by period statement that lists all the costs payable during construction phase followed by a statement listing the parties financing these costs in each model period. This is called "sources and uses of funds statement during construction".

Uses of funds

Again, a uses of funds statement should contain all the costs payable during construction.

The following are examples of the major uses or expense categories:

Table 4: Sample Uses Statement.

USES	Period 1	Period 2
Developmental Costs		
Development fees		
Construction/Capital Expenditure Costs		
Contractor Costs /EPC costs		
Non-Contractor Costs /Non-EPC costs		
Pre-funding of reserve accounts		
Prefunding of working capital account		
Pre-funding of maintenance reserve account		
Contingency Costs		
Financing Fees		
Interest during construction		
Financial fees (Commitment, front-end, appraisal, supervision fees …)		
Pre-funding of debt service reserve account		
TOTAL		

Sources of Funds

The sources statement, should simply states who will pay for the costs.

Table 5: Sample Sources Statement

SOURCES	Period 1	Period 2
Debt		
Development Banks		
Commercial Banks		
Subordinated debt		
Equity		
Pure Equity		
Shareholder loan		
TOTAL		

Sources = Uses

The total amount of sources in each model period should equal the total amount of uses in the corresponding model period.

In the same manner, total uses of funds should equal total sources of funds.

Make sure that these periodic and sum total checks are included in the model.

Summary Sources and Uses

Since sources and uses of funds is an important statement, it is good to include a summary sources and uses in the summary sheet (dashboard).

The following are examples of the summary sources and uses of funds:

Circular reference in Sources and uses of funds

If you recall from season 1, we said that you want to avoid intentional or unintentional circular reference in the financial model. A good example of inevitable circular reference is in the sources and uses of funds statement.

As you saw in the uses of funds, there are financing costs which depend on the size of the debt and typically in project finance deals, debt is sized using a fixed debt to capital ratio. In other words, debt itself is a function of total project cost and here goes the evil circular reference.

 Total project cost = Construction cost + Debt * interest rate

Debt = %x * Total Project Cost

Figure 28: Circular Reference

To deal with this issue, there are different options:

• If the project is in an advanced stage where the term sheets with the lenders are signed, then the model can use a hard-coded input for debt and therefore there will be no circularity in the model. However, if this agreement is not reached yet, even if there are 10 lenders and all 9 lenders have signed their term sheet but one is remaining floating, then you should not fix the debt amount.

• Iterative model. This makes the model unstable and it is not recommended.

• Copy and paste macro: This is a common method used in project finance model, but it significantly reduces the financial model functionality.

• User defined function. This is a method developed by Professor Edward Bodmer. It is the best method that solves for circularity and doesn't negatively impact the model functionality. The details of this method are beyond the scope of this work.

How I stopped being a "copy-paster"

• I started building and working on Excel-based models in 2008 when I was an economics PhD candidate and working as a trainer for the executive training program of Queen's University. At the time, the models were mostly designed for training purposes. My focus was mainly the cost and benefit analysis of investment projects, rather than their financial analysis. In 2010, Professor Glenn Jenkins selected me to be part of his team of consultants at the African Development Bank (AfDB). That's when I had to face and model complex issues like debt sizing, debt service reserve accounts, different tranches of debt and equity, shareholder loans, cash sweeps, guarantee support programs and other complications. At the same time, I also had to deal with circularity in spreadsheets.

• The first financial model that I built for the AfDB was the lenders' financial model for Abidjan's 'Third Bridge' project. This project had all manner of complications, including circular references as you might imagine. I knew that I could not let the circularity run

freely in my model, so that was when I wrote my first VBA code (a copy and paste code with a loop). I remember I was so excited and proud of the end result and I even added a flashy button and named it 'optimization' in a summary sheet I named 'dashboard'!

• This method worked for some time and I was happy with my copy-and-paste macro. However, as I started working on more complex issues like bid models and revenue-guarantee structures; I noticed that the copy-and-paste macro was limiting my models. Trust me, when every time you change an input, your model copies and pastes multiple rows repeatedly (and runs a goal seek simultaneously) and it will take quite a while. If you are patient, you might be fine working with this model yourself, but we usually use these models during contract negotiations and have to run scenarios live during meetings. While the model is running, you have either to endure the awkward silence in the room or to engage in small talk about the weather!

• When facing a problem, you can seek a solution yourself or find someone who has found a solution. For me that someone was Edward Bodmer. I had been following Edward's work for years. While everyone else was watching Game of Thrones, I was watching Edward's video tutorials on YouTube. I was desperate to adopt his method and get rid of the copy and paste macro I was once so proud of. Having tried several times and failed, it was only last year that I had the chance of one-on-one training with Edward Bodmer. Finally, I could learn some of his tricks.

• There have been two turning points in my life. First was having Lasik eye surgery that let me see without my thick glasses. Second was meeting Edward Bodmer. He opened my eyes to a new horizon in financial Excel modelling.

• Bodmer's technique applies user-defined functions to solve any circular reference problem in Excel. In this method, you need to reprogram in VBA the equations causing circularity in the financial model, and then use this function in the Excel model. This method not only makes your model more flexible and faster; it also helps you to debug your models. This is because you are basically programming the same calculations twice: once in Excel and once in VBA. Most times the mistakes are in your Excel formulae rather than in the VBA code!

• For more on that subject, I refer you to the creator himself and strongly recommend that you take a course with him to learn his techniques and to be introduced to the future of financial modelling.

www.financeenergyinstitute.com

edbodmer.com

SEASON 3, EPISODE 2 ▶
Financial model detective, integrated financial statements

Now that you have reviewed all the pieces of the puzzle, you can go and have a look at the big picture. The big picture comes in the form of integrated financial statements.

Income Statement

The following are the main accounts that need to be covered when projecting income statement line items:

By including all of the above (and more if necessary), you can arrive at net income, or bottom line of the income statement.

REVENUE

OPEX

DEPRECIATION EXPENSE

INTEREST EXPENSE

TAX EXPENSE

Below is a screenshot from one of an income statement forecast.

	E	F	M	N	O	P
1	AFS					
2	Total Model Errors	OK				
3	Active Scenario	Base Case				
4						
5	Model period beginning	flag	01 Jan 21	01 Jan 22	01 Jan 23	01 Jan 24
6	Model period ending	flag	31 Dec 21	31 Dec 22	31 Dec 23	31 Dec 24
52	**PROFIT AND LOSS STATEMENT IN MILLION USD**					
54	Total Operating Revenues	million USD	8.1	8.1	8.1	8.1
55	Total Operating Expenses	million USD	(1.7)	(1.7)	(1.8)	(1.8)
56	Cost of heavy maintenance	million USD	(0.1)	(0.1)	(0.1)	(0.1)
57	Developer Fee payable during Ops	million USD	-	-	-	-
58	EBITDA	million USD	6.29	6.23	6.16	6.11
60	Depreciation expenses	million USD	(2.5)	(2.5)	(2.5)	(2.5)
61	EBIT	million USD	3.8	3.7	3.7	3.6
63	DSRA LC	million USD	(0.0)	(0.0)	(0.0)	(0.0)
64	Senior Debt Interest payments during ops	million USD	(1.8)	(1.7)	(1.5)	(1.4)
65	EBT	million USD	2.00	2.03	2.07	2.13
67	Corporate Tax charge due and paid	million USD	(0.6)	(0.6)	(0.6)	(0.6)
68	NPAT	million USD	1.4	1.4	1.4	1.5
70	Dividends Paid before WHT	million USD	(1.3)	(1.9)	(1.8)	(1.7)
71	Retained Earnings	million USD	0.1	(0.4)	(0.3)	(0.2)
73	Retained Earnings BEG	million USD	-	0.1	(0.4)	(0.7)
74	Retained Earnings END	million USD	0.1	(0.4)	(0.7)	(0.9)
75						
76	**BALANCE SHEET MILLION USD**					
77						
78	**Assets**					

InputC | InputS | Sens | IFS | AFS | Summary | Check | TimePreOps | Dev | Capex | ConsFin | Ti ...

Figure 30: Income statement forecast

Balance sheet

In a project finance model, you might not necessarily need a balance sheet during the appraisal stage, but you better have it. Why?

• When modelling, you never think short-term. You should consider this model is a tool that accompanies the project throughout its life cycle. It will go through structural changes however, you want to make sure that the key elements are included, and balance sheet is one the key elements.

• Balance sheet helps you to reconcile things and debug the model. A balance sheet that does not balance might be headache to fix but along the way you will catch mistakes in the model.

• Financial model auditor will ask for it.

	E	F	M	N	O	P	Q	R
1	AFS							
2	Total Model Errors	OK						
3	Active Scenario	Base Case						
4								
5	Model period beginning	flag	01 Jan 21	01 Jan 22	01 Jan 23	01 Jan 24	01 Jan 25	01 Jan 26
6	Model period ending	flag	31 Dec 21	31 Dec 22	31 Dec 23	31 Dec 24	31 Dec 25	31 Dec 26
7	Year End	Year	2021	2022	2023	2024	2025	20
76	**BALANCE SHEET MILLION USD**							
78	**Assets**							
79	Accounts Receivable Balances END	million USD	0.67	0.66	0.66	0.66	0.66	0.
80	DSRA Balance END	million USD	0.00	0.00	0.00	0.00	0.00	0.
81	Retained Cash Balance END	million USD	0.10	0.10	0.10	0.10	0.09	0.
82	Current Assets	million USD	0.77	0.8	0.8	0.8	0.7	0
84	Net Fixed Asset Balance END	million USD	47.63	45.12	42.61	40.11	37.60	35.
85	Long Term Assets	million USD	47.63	45.1	42.6	40.1	37.6	35
87	Total Assets	million USD	48.40	45.9	43.4	40.9	38.3	35
89	**Liabilities**							
90	Account Payable Balances END	million USD	0.14	0.14	0.15	0.15	0.15	0.
91	Current Liabilities	million USD	0.14	0.1	0.1	0.1	0.2	0
93	Senior Debt 1 Balance END	million USD	28.16	26.40	24.56	22.62	20.58	18.
94	Senior Debt 2 Balance END	million USD	4.97	4.66	4.33	3.99	3.63	3.
95	Long Term Liabilities	million USD	33.13	31.1	28.9	26.6	24.2	21
97	Total Liabilities	million USD	33.27	31.2	29.0	26.8	24.4	21
99	**Equity**							
100	Equity Balance END	million USD	15.04	15.04	15.04	15.04	15.04	15.
101	Retained Earnings END	million USD	0.09	-0.36	-0.70	-0.94	-1.05	-1.
102	Total Equity	million USD	15.13	14.7	14.3	14.1	14.0	14
104	Balance Sheet Check	0.00	0.00	0.00	0.00	0.00	0.00	0.
105			Ok	Ok	Ok	Ok	Ok	Ok

| ◀ ▶ ... | InputC | InputS | Sens | IFS | **AFS** | Summary | Check | TimePreOps | Dev | Capex | ConsFin | Ti ... ⊕ ⋮ |

Figure 31: Balance sheet statement forecast

Cash flow waterfall

The final core component of the financial model is the cash flow waterfall statement. A proper cash waterfall indicates the seniority and subordination of various cash flow items. The cash waterfall will be documented in loan documentation.

FiNEXMOD

THE ONLY PLACE WHERE IT PAYS OFF TO BE AT THE BOTTOM IS THE BOTTOM OF A CASH FLOW WATERFALL

Screenshot below is a high-level illustration of a typical cash flow waterfall.

	Units	01 Jan 19 30 Jun 19 Cons	01 Jul 19 31 Dec 19 Cons	01 Jan 20 30 Jun 20 Cons	01 Jul 20 31 Dec 20 Cons	01 Jan 21 30 Jun 21 Ops	01 Jul 21 31 Dec 21 Ops
Total Model Errors	OK						
Active Scenario	Base Case						
Model period beginning	flag						
Model period ending	flag						
Timeline Label	Units						
CASHFLOW WATERFALL IN MILLION USD							
Cash received from operations	million USD	-	-	-	-	3.37	4.10
Cash Paid for operation	million USD	-	-	-	-	(0.70)	(0.86)
Cost of heavy maintenance	million USD	-	-	-	-	(0.07)	(0.07)
Developer Fee-total	million USD	(4.90)	-	-	-	-	-
EPC -total	million USD	(23.48)	(6.14)	(3.63)	(2.57)	-	-
Other Costs-total	million USD	(5.37)	(0.44)	(0.26)	(0.18)	-	-
Pre-Tax Cash Flow from Operations	million USD	(33.76)	(6.57)	(3.89)	(2.76)	2.5984	3.17
Corporate Tax charge due and paid	million USD	-	-	-	-	(0.29)	(0.31)
Cashflow Before Funding	million USD	(33.76)	(6.57)	(3.89)	(2.76)	2.31	2.86
Equity Drawdowns	million USD	15	-	-	-	-	-
Senior Debt 1 drawdown	million USD	17	6.2	4	3	-	-
Senior Debt 2 drawdown	million USD	3	1	1	1	-	-
Cashflow Available for Senior Debt Service (CFADS)	million USD	0.86	0.66	0.77	0.86	2.31	2.86
Senior Debt 1 Fees	million USD	(0)	(0.1)	(0)	(0)	-	-
Senior Debt 1 Interest payments during cons	million USD	(0)	(0.5)	(1)	(1)	-	-
Senior Debt 1 Interest payments during Ops during ops	million USD	-	-	-	-	(1)	(1)
Senior Debt 1 Principal repayment	million USD	-	-	-	-	(1)	(1)
Senior Debt 2 Fees	million USD	(0)	(0.0)	(0)	(0)	-	-
Senior Debt 2 Interest payments during cons	million USD	(0)	(0.1)	(0)	(0)	-	-
Senior Debt 2 Interest payments during	million USD	-	-	-	-	(0)	(0)
Senior Debt 2 Principal repayment	million USD	-	-	-	-	(0)	(0)
DSRA LC	million USD	-	-	-	-	(0)	(0)
Cashflow Available for DSRA	million USD	0.00	0.00	0.00	0.00	0.43	0.98
Pre-funding of DSRA amount	million USD	-	-	-	-	-	-
Funding of DSRA from Cashflow	million USD	-	-	-	-	-	-
Release Excess Funds in DSRA	million USD	-	-	-	-	-	-
Release from DSRA to Fund a cash Shortfall	million USD	-	-	-	-	-	-
Cashflow Available for Equity	million USD	0.00	0.00	0.00	0.00	0.43	0.98
Cash Calls	million USD	-	-	-	-	-	-
Dividends Paid before WHT	million USD	-	-	-	-	(0.39)	(0.92)
Movement in Cash	million USD	0.00	0.00	0.00	0.00	0.04	0.06
Retained Cash Balance BEG	million USD	-	0.00	0.00	0.00	0.00	0.04
Less Excess Funding	million USD	-	-	-	-	-	-
Retained Cash Balance END	million USD	0.00	0.00	0.00	0.00	0.04	0.10
Min Retained Cash Balance Check							
Min Retained Cash Balance	million USD						
Min Retained Cash Balance Check	flag						

Figure 33: High level illustration of a typical cash flow waterfall

Charts:

Visualize the data in charts and observe the trend in different items in the financial statement. By observing the trends, you might come up with additional questions and can go back and check the underlying assumptions.

Periodicity of financial statement:

In season 2, we talked about the choice and the periodicity of the model. In terms of presentation, the financial statements can be presented in the chosen model periodicity and aggregated to annual for presentation purpose. For example, if the model is built on semi-annual basis, the financial statement will be presented on semi-annual basis and having annual financial statement from semi-annual flows will also be useful.

Necessary checks:

• Balance sheet should balance.

• There should not be any negative cashflows in any given period.

Return and ratios

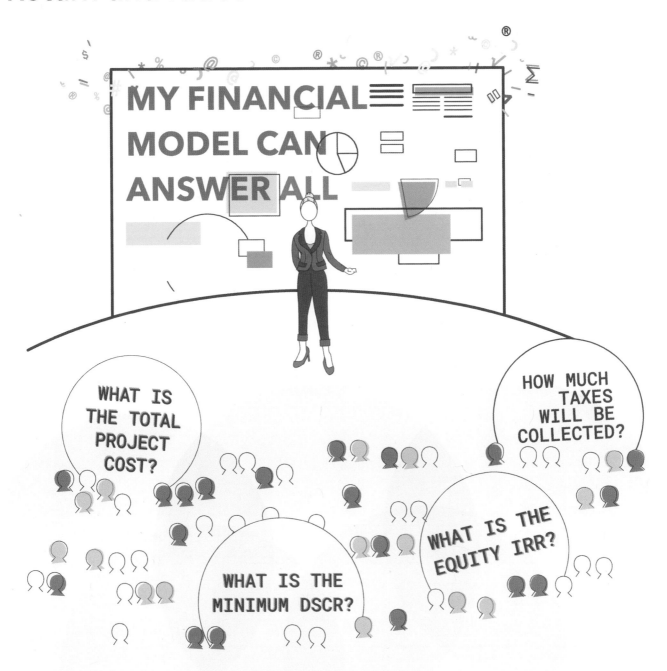

The financial model should contain summary metrics that speak to different stakeholders. Most probably you have heard and even calculated these metrics hundred times in your life and sometime when we say the equity IRR is 15%, everyone is familiar with the expression but maybe we don't exactly grasp what it means. So it is always good to think like a novice and revise our basic concepts. Here are some of the basic metrics that are typically included in a project finance financial model:

Lenders and Credit analysis

Lenders main concern is whether the future cash flows of the project are sufficient to fund operating costs and the debt service? The following metrics can answer these questions:

DSCR – debt service coverage ratio.

DSCR measures the ability to pay the debt in any particular payment period.

$$DSCR = \frac{[CFADS \text{ over Loan Life}(t)]}{[\text{Principal repayment }(t) + \text{Interest repayment }(t)]}.$$

A DSCR ratio of 1.00x means that the cash is just sufficient to pay for the debt service.

A ratio less than 1.00x indicates that there is insufficient cash to pay for the current debt service.

A ratio of 1.30x that for a total debt service due of $ 100 the free cash flow available to service the same is $ 130. In other words the cash flow can fall by 23% before the project company is unable to service its debt. So if someone tell you that the min DSCR is 1.25x you can conclude that there is 20% ((1.25 – 1)/1.25 =20%) buffer in the cash flow.

LLCR - loan life coverage ratio.

The LLCR is defined as the ratio of the net present value of cash flow available for debt service for the outstanding life of the debt to the outstanding debt amount. It is a break-even ratio. It measures by how much the cash flow with restructuring can go down and the loan can still be paid by the end of the loan life ability of the borrower to repay an outstanding loan.

LLCR = PV [CFADS over Loan Life] / PV(Debt Service)
The discount rate used in the net present value (NPV) calculation is typically the weighted average cost of debt.

The CFADS in the denominator of the LLCR is from commercial operation date (COD), and up to end of the loan life.

An LLCR of 2.00x means that the CFADS, on a discounted basis, is double the amount of the outstanding debt balance or in other words the project achieves a break-even LLCR at 50% reduction of the base case cash flows.

PLCR - Project life coverage ratio
The PLCR is similar to the LLCR – but it is calculated over the life of the project (LLCR is calculated over the life of the loan).
If something goes wrong and there is a need for restructuring of the debt, this ratio tells the debt service capacity beyond the final maturity of the loan.

Return Analysis

Equity IRR

Measure of the underlying return the private sector expects to achieve by investing in the project.

Mathematically, it is defined as the discount rate which, when applied to investor's net cash flows, returns a net present value (NPV) of zero.

Think of it as the constant interest rate at which a given series of cash outflows must be invested in order for the investor to earn a given series of cash inflows as income.

What's more important is what is included in this return. So always trace back the IRR calculation and look at the cash flow component.

How to handle development capital in calculation of equity IRR? That is an important question to ask when reviewing the return. As we said in the CapEx and S&U discussion, we discussed about the development capital and development capital fee. Now if the developer is also the equity provider, then for the return

calculation, you should consider the cash flow from development phase up to decommissioning. For example, if the developer had spent USD 2 million since 2017 to get the project to closing and then it will need to put an additional USD 10 million during construction with the expectation of getting a 120 kUSD per year under a 5 year fixed contract, then you can actually calculated 2 Equity IRRs:

Equity IRR at FC: meaning from financial close onwards. Then the cash flow to consider in the IRR will be 15%.

Table 6: IRR calculation at
financial close.

Year		2017	2018	2019	2020	2021	2022	2023
Net Cash flow	mUSD	0.00	-10.00	2.98	2.98	2.98	2.98	2.98
IRR@FC	%	15.00%						

Now you want to tell the investor how much is the all-in return meaning starting from development stage and considering the development capital spent and the development fees earned. In the same example, let's say that the sponsor at financial close will cash in 1.50 x fees on their development capital, and then the all-in IRR will be almost 18%.

Table 6: Life cycle IRR calculation including
development phase

Year		2017	2018	2019	2020	2021	2022	2023
Net Cash flow	mUSD	0.00	-10.00	2.98	2.98	2.98	2.98	2.98
less: Development capital	mUSD	2.00	0.00	0.00	0.00	0.00	0.00	0.00
Plus:Development fee	mUSD	0.00	3.00	0.00	0.00	0.00	0.00	0.00
Net cash flow including development	mUSD	-2.00	-7.00	2.98	2.98	2.98	2.98	2.98
IRR	%	17.87%						

Important side note is for the bid models when you are for example using the equity IRR for setting the price, then you might want to consider what IRR should be used as the reference in the analysis.

If you have multiple shareholders and you want to know how much each shareholder is earning, then you need to do a separate IRR calculation for each shareholder. The return might be identical if they only have differences in shareholding is SPV however if any of the below then their return will be different:

• Tax implications: their dividends or shareholder returns might be subject to different tax rate depending on where they are coming from.

• If there are any sort of free-carry structure.

• Any inter shareholder loan.

• Different timing of injections.

Equity NPV

Net present value is the current worth of a future sum of money or stream of cash flows at a certain discount rate (time value of money).

For the choice of discount rate, it is mainly company-specific as it's linked to how the company gets its funds.

For every IRR that you calculate in the model, you can also calculate the corresponding NPV.

Pay-back period

This metrics calculates when will shareholders make back the investment they put in.
It can be expressed as date or number of year.

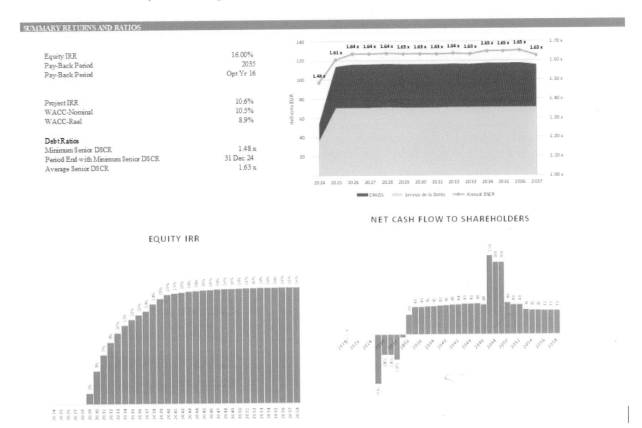

Figure 35: Screenshot of summary sheet

Sensitivity and scenario analysis

The financial model is eventually a tool that should enable you perform different type of analysis on the inputs and results. Normally, any typical project finance model already includes sensitivity parameters and some sort of presentation of sensitivity and scenario results. If the model does not include any sensitivity analysis, then you can easily have it built in the model. Here are some of the typical methods:

1. Sensitivity using data table

Step 1: define the sensitivity parameters.

Step 2: define the range of deviation from the base case estimate.

Step 3: set up the data table in one way or two-way table and use the Data Table under "What If" analysis to run sensitivities.

However, if you have copy and paste macro then you will not be able to use the data Table functionality. You will then need to create another copy and paste macro with a loop to run sensitivities and copy and paste values after any incremental change in the target input.

2. Scenario analysis

One approach is to separate the constant inputs from time base inputs and reflect the constant inputs in scenario analysis style. This way we can effectively define different scenarios. Some of the typical scenarios are:

Sponsor base case/ Sponsor down case / Sponsor up case

Lenders base case/ Lenders down case/ Lenders up case

Authority base case/ Authority down case/ Authority up care

Base case with tax exemptions/ Base case without tax exemptions

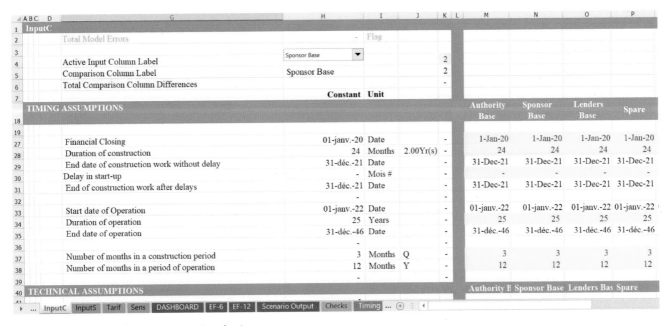

Figure 36: Multiple Scenario Analysis

No matter what side of the story you are, make sure that you understand and test the model under different scenario. Again as we said before, being in project finance deal is like dealing with a family business, we are all in it together and the interest of each party might be different from each other but if the deal is not win win for all parties, there will be problems for all. So if you are on the sponsor's side, check the model under different lenders scenario and see whether the project is still viable looking from lenders, and same for government side.

Q&A

Congratulation! You have finished your first round of financial model review. Now you are ready to draft a list of questions on the financial model.

Usually the questions and answers related to the model are done either on the body of an email or it is sent in a word document.

In my experience, it is more efficient to keep track of all Q&As related to the model in a separate sheet within the corresponding model and keep this sheet throughout the due diligence process.

This is useful for internal discussions and also when you receive comments on the model from the model auditor or any other third party.

This is in line with the principal of transparency and also it is an efficient way to keep track of any comment received on the model.

Here's a screenshot of a sample Q&A sheet.

	A	B	C	D	E	F	G	H
1	QA							
2		The status of issues are classified as follows:						
3								
4		Open			The issue is yet to be resolved			
5		Closed			The issue has been resolved			
6			C/F		The issue is carried forward pending for further information			
8		Issues arising from this review are classified as follows:						
9		High			1 – High, e.g., potential error which may require a significant model adjustment			
10		Medium			2 – Medium, e.g., other issue of concern but expected to be of lower impact			
11		Low			3 – Low, e.g., presentational or expected to be a low impact issue.			
12								
13		Matters arising from review of Financial Model Filename: "Q&A_FinancialModel_Audit example.xlsx"						

N	Impact Level	Status	Category	Reference	Question/comment
1		Open	Model mechanics	opex, Row 11	There are a number of long nested if formulas, for the ease of audit and simplicity, please break these formulas .
2		Open	Error checks		It is useful to add additional checks other than the ones already included.
3		Open	Macros		Macros are password protected. Could you please send us the password so that we could review the macro codes.
6		Open	EPC	Inputs Cell F55	the detailed breakdown of EPC is not included. If at this stage the breakdown is not yet available, however the model should accommodate that so that once we have the EPC contract, we could include the general items in the model.
8		Open	EPC	Inputs Cell F55	Total project cost seems to be on the low range. Could you please clarify what are the competitive advantages that you have identified that are resulting in a cost lower than similar project of the same nature.
9		Open	Contingency	Inputs Cell F59	3% contingency is low. Lenders usually require at least 5% of total project cost as contingency.
10		Open	Taxes	Capex Rows 124 to 166	Is the project exempted from VAT, import duties and any other taxes during construction? Please provide reference.

The next section is a list of question and answer extracted from real project discussions. I should thank Andrey Kelvchuk here for the work on extracting most of this information which I used his work as the base for the preparation of this list.

APPENDIX
REAL EXAMPLES
OF FINANCIAL
MODEL ISSUE LIST

I. MODEL MECHANICS AND STRUCTURE

1. Model does not have a proper structure, nor defined set of revenues, set of opex projections and a proper cash waterfall and it's very confusing to figure out seniority and subordination of various cash flow items.

2. Why is it that there is no summary sheet in the model to present key results and outcomes of the project, to summarize the benefits to the equity holders and the capability indicators of the project to pay back the loan?

3. The model has been presented without firm dates on Financial Close, Notice to Proceed and Commercial Operations Date.

4. The model has spelling mistakes.

5. Why is it that the financial model does not have the "Sources and Uses of funds table"?

6. Term-sheet lending terms and conditions are not reflected in the current Model.

7. Model is rather engineering-oriented.

8. Hidden worksheets.

9. Hardcoded figures throughout the model.

10. Could you please indicate what the hard-coded figures included within the formulas in these cells represent? For the purpose of transparency and flexibility, please include all hard-coded figures in "Inputs" with proper labelling and unit of measurements.

11. Empty rows with no computations. If not required, kindly remove.

12. Formula in this row is untitled, refers to empty cells and is not used anywhere in the model. If not require, delete.

13. This sheet is blank but there are references to it. If it is not required kindly delete it?

14. Unused cells - should be removed from the model?

15. The formulas are long. Consider breaking out the long formulas to make them easier to understand

16. There are no sanity checks included in the model. The sanity checks serve as a quick indicator of a material data inconsistency in the model.

17. The macros run correctly, however, the use of the macros have led to input of hardcoded numbers in the model.

18. The colour coding is not consistently used in the model.

19. The formula is linked incorrectly.

20. The units of measurements were not clearly stated and used through out the model. We recommend dedicating a column in each worksheet for units of measurements.

21. The quarterly projections adequately reflect projected estimates. However The model does not build up into an annual model. The lack of annualized numbers makes it difficult to see the Company's performance at the end of each year.

II. INVESTMENT COSTS / CAPEX

22. Capex figures in the financial model are different from the figures in the Project Information Memorandum (PIM). Please clarify which figures are up to date and should be used for the analysis.

23. Are the Capex figures adjusted for inflation? In other words, are they in nominal terms?.

24. The "Development Costs", "Construction Costs" and "Other Costs" are calculated in the real terms and not in the nominal terms. This is unexpected. Please confirm that this is as intended.

25. Could you provide additional details on "Other costs"?.

26. What is included in "construction management fees"? Who pays this? Who is the recipient? What activities are funded? .

27. A success fee of 1% was provided. The source of data is not available to assess its adequacy and accuracy. Please indicate which party is the recipient? What activities are funded?.

28. A development premium of 5% was provided. The source of data is not available to assess its adequacy and accuracy. The supporting documentation confirming the figures provided are required.

29. Could you provide additional information on the "Other financing costs" elements?.

30. Inputs sheet, lime 68. "interests on development bridge loan". Why 'bridge loan'? Isn't it development premium?.

31. How are the capital costs spread (semi-annually or quarterly) over this construction period?.

32. How long (in months) is the actual construction period, starting from the financial close?.

33. The Contract Price in the EPC Terms Sheet is €Xm. However in the Model it is €Ym. Please confirm this is agreed and that it will populated in the next version of the EPC Terms Sheet.

34. The definition of Payment in the EPC Terms Sheet states that the contractor is entitled to get an advance payment of [15%] of the Contract Price. However in the Model, the contractor get an advance of 5% in March 2018 and the remaining 10% in July 2018. Please review/explain.

35. The clause xx of the EPC Contract defines that the payment will be made after 30 days of receiving the invoice. However in the Model, the EPC cost is assumed to be paid in the same month in which it is accrued. Please review /explain this discrepancy.

36. The EPC Terms Sheets defines the liquidated damages, however the amounts are not present in the Model. We understand that it will not be a part of the Base Case but can be required to be in the Model while running the construction delay sensitivities. Please review/explain as to why liquidated damages are not included in the Model.

37. How much costs have been spent up to date? What is the status of construction of the first plant: civil works; equipment installation and testing? What amount has been spent up to date, and on what activities/assets?.

38. Please kindly provide us with a capex plan as well as a pre-opex plan before completion. How has the bridge-loan been used?.

39. There are fixed operating costs during construction? Would fixed cost be incurred during construction period!?.

40. Opening expenses of USD XXX mln. Provide detailed list of opening expenses; provide amounts and time when such expenses are expected to happen.

41. Why is the initial balance of the minimum cash of USD XXX million not part of project costs?.

42. Provide a list of items/activities procured locally.

43. How were "miscellaneous costs" / "other costs" estimated? Provide detailed break-down.

44. What's included in "development costs"? Provide details and detailed breakdown.

45. What's included in "development premium" / "Sponsor's premium"? Provide details and detailed breakdown. How this has been estimated?

46. What's included in "Owners G&A costs"?

47. Financing, legal and EIA costs of USD XX million and Development Cost of USD XXX million – what is the source/reference for these extra costs? Why these costs are not included in project costs and financing plan? Why not included in cashflows?

48. "A number of new roads will have to be built to provide access to the project...." Should the necessary road(s) upgrade costs near the site be part of the project? If the project does not upgrade the road(s), who will?

49. The road construction is a significant infrastructure/parameter of the project, just as mentioned in the Business Plan. However, its cost has not been clearly defined and reflected in the project cost structure. It is also not clear who will pay for the road.

50. What's the status of relocation and compensation? Has it been negotiated with the affected households and community? Who is responsible for compensation and relocation? Have all related costs been included in the model? What's the total value of relocation and compensation costs? Does the valuation of the compensation package include the loss of income for the displaced?

51. "It appears that the total investment cost is under-estimated by at least XXX million, because:

• Model assume the cost of senior debt at about x% (LIBOR of y% + margin of z%), while both LIBOR rate and the margin are likely to increase;

• Model assume pro-rata drawdown of equity and debt, while Lenders demand that equity is to be spent first;

• When equity is spent first, commitment fees will increase but interest during construction will reduce somewhat;

• DSRA is not included in model, while initial seed funding for a 6-month DSRA about XXX mln;

• This under-estimation does not include any contingencies of cost-overrun facilities that Lenders typically require for project of this type.

52. Are there any withholding taxes on construction contracts by local and foreign contractors?

53. Taxes during construction are considered as capex, and hence should, in principle, be amortizable. However, legal advisor advised that some taxes are not amortizable and provided the amount of these, to exclude them from depreciations.

54. What items of investment costs are subject to import duty? At what rate? What is the total amount of import duty? Is import duty amount already included in the figures presented?

55. What items of investment costs are subject to VAT? At what rate? What is the total amount of VAT? Is VAT amount already included in the figures presented? If VAT is refunded – what is the processing time and realistic delay in receiving the refunds?

56. Please confirm if contingency cost items represent the physical and price escalation in capex over the construction period.

57. Contingency of x% of EPC value. Low. When the cost estimates were made? Has the supplier quotation increased since?

58. Contingency provision of xx%: why such a high rate?

59. There is too much contingency provision for the capital cost structure; xx% on EPC costs and xx% on other capital costs excluding EPC costs.

60. The contingency is embedded in the overall costs and cannot be identified as a separate item in their model. Could you please indicate what is the contingency included in the financing and construction costs?

61. Why is the amount of contingency set at such a low value of x% of construction costs when we normally expect to see at least xx%?

62. EPC contract is shown as a single item and single lump-sum amount. Provide a full breakdown of activities and costs under the Building and Equipment EPC Contracts.

63. It's not clear why additional insurance coverage is needed for construction activities if the construction is carried out on fixed price and fixed time basis?

64. States that the EPC contract does not cover the risks associated with major unforeseen events or changes in project's scope, furthermore the financial model does not provide for any cost overrun on EPC Capex, how are the increases in EPC due to these unforeseen events and changes in the project scope mitigated?

65. EPC liquidated damages due and payable by the project have not been modeled. There is need to fully understand the extent of the contingent liability.

66. Considering the fact that this is could be considered as an EPCM contract, not EPC contract, do the sponsors have the financial ability to inject further equity to cover the possible cost overruns?

67. Cost-overrun facilities that Lenders typically require for project of this type. How are cost-overruns and/or delays going to be covered? Suggest to set-up a stand-by facility of xx% of total investment costs with preferably 100% equity [or x% equity and y% debt] to provide a dis-incentive to use it. Pricing of facility must be more expensive than senior debt.

68. There is a difference of EUR XXX million between the Sources and Uses of finance. How will this be funded?

69. What's the nature and purpose of Letter(s) of Credit? Does project pay for these LCs? Why these costs are not part of investment costs?

70. Why are grants included as negative assets? Would it be required for tax purposes? What does the tax law says about treatment of investment grants?

71. Capex do not change with delays. Is it realistic to assume so bearing in mind that Capex, taxes and IDCs are subject to fluctuations?

72. Will the government be responsible to build and maintain/operate the associated infrastructure? Has the government currently budgeted for this expenditure?

III. OPEX

73. There is need for a clear breakdown of the operating and maintenance costs by item, by period.

74. provide a list of items/activities procured locally. Indicate the amounts spent. What is the breakdown of local versus foreign costs of the project?

75. Fixed amount (in nominal terms) of O&M over time. Should then O&M expenses be revised? The plant and project infrastructure will require regular maintenance and replacements, and this should increase O&M costs over time of operation.

76. Are these fixed operating costs (not variable costs) during construction? Would fixed cost be incurred during construction period!?

77. How were "miscellaneous costs" / "other costs" estimated? Provide detailed break-down.

78. What is included in "Technical Assistance"? Who pays this? Who is the recipient? What activities are funded? Is this item included in project Opex?

79. Why is the gas price indexed to US dollar, not to local or Euro?

80. Marketing fee: what's the base and the rate of the fee? The fee increases from USD XXX to XXXX million per annum. is this size of the fee justified?

81. O&M provide number of employees by project unit; by skill level; gross salaries; net salaries; indicate the rates and amounts of taxes, social security contributions, bonuses, etc. Indicate the number of local and expatriate employees. What is the assumed growth rate in real wages (in excess of the general rate of inflation)?

82. What personal income tax rates are applied to different labor categories employed by the project?

83. Are the project's local employees required to make social security contributions? If yes, what is the level required? Project is required to make such contributions on behalf of the local employees.

84. The local staff for the project would require extensive training and that O&M Plan provides for this training program; how much is the training costs and are they included in the financial model?

85. What are the applicable tax regulations and policies (e.g VAT, import duties, other taxes, subsidies, etc) that the project will be subject to?

86. What operating items are subject to import duties, excise taxes or VAT? Have these taxes been properly included?

87. Is water and electricity exempted from sales tax or any other tax? Water and electricity prices are not subject to taxes as these are included in the tariff.

88. O&M costs seem to be too low. Specifically, O&M variable cost of 0.005 $/kwh is x times lower as compared to variable O&M cost of similar project.

IV. MAINTENANCE

89. Annual Routine Maintenance and Annual Rehabilitation costs are zero?

90. Project does not have any maintenance capex at all? Is that possible? is it fair to say that over the next x years there will never be any maintenance activities?

91. Fixed amount (in nominal terms) for O&M over time. Should then O&M expenses be revised? The plant and project infrastructure will require regular maintenance and replacements, and this should increase O&M costs over time of operation.

92. What is the duration of major scheduled maintenance?

93. No provision for the Maintenance Reserve Account is currently made. Can you confirm how maintenance requirements will be provided for?

V. REVENUES / REVENUE DURING CONSTRUCTION

94. What's the currency of invoicing and billing?

95. It is observed that the revenues decrease over time, please explain why this is so?

96. Could you elaborate on the reasons why a constant price decline of x% (or less) during x years seems reasonable to you? Could you explain how this would be feasible in light of the competition that you expect?

97. Volume projection used in base case is the highest among the 5 scenarios available. Why this projection is taken as the base case?

98. Why is the inflation on tariffs higher than inflation on costs?

99. The revenues during construction will be obtained over x months, from month y to month z. The project starts repaying the loan principal in month xx into construction period of xx months. If the revenues during construction are not realized as planned, this will have negative impact on repayment of the debt during construction and affect the viability of the project.

100. Collection of potential Revenue during Construction is assumed 100%, which is very optimistic. Suggest lowering this figure.

101. How will the debt service during construction be repaid if the revenues during construction are not realized as planned?

102. Interest Income rate of x% is high. It's very surprising that interest income is significantly higher that interest paid.

103. The interest rate in calculation of interest income is quite high. Currently 6-months LIBOR is approximately x%. Usually, sight deposits carry an interest rate of Libor minus x%. This source of income should not be relied on and included as source of fund as it is highly dependent on the market conditions which are unpredictable. Secondly, its amount is currently x% of total funding requirements. For clarity we would recommend to not include this item in the sources of funds.

104. Is the project charging VAT on its output? If yes, at what rate? Is VAT refundable? If VAT is levied, how quickly does the project receive a VAT refund - is there a delay? How many months?

VI. WORKING CAPITAL

105. Following working capital assumption are taken into consideration :

• No delay in the payment of Development Costs, Construction Costs, Other Costs.

• 30 days delay in the payment of Operating expenses.

• 40 days delay in the receiving of Operating revenues.
 Please confirm that this is as intended.

106. Could you specify whether or not you have working cash requirements, why or why not, and, if so, how they are taken into account?

107. Cashflows do not have any provision for working capital. Receivables and inventories (especially with VAT) are typically very significant. Model is over-optimistic about its cash receipts.

108. Fuel costs and debtors days (??) at 60 appear to be high. A 30 day facility is more realistic.

109. How was the "working capital loan" amount determined, and where will it be sourced from?

110. In the calculating the Accounts Payable, why are fuel, raw material, and spares treated separately from the Accounts Payable?

111. Why is cash balance not treated as part of working capital requirement in the WC sheet?

112. Please indicate why minimum cash balance is not released at operation end date? And is it financed as part of project cost?

VII. TAXES

113. What are the applicable tax regulations and policies (e.g VAT, import duties, other taxes, subsidies, etc) that the project will be subject to?

114. What items of investment costs are subject to import duty? At what rate? What is the total amount of import duty? Is import duty amount already included in the figures presented?

115. For each of the capex item in the below, please provide level of taxes and any other tariffs that the project has to pay.

116. Are there any withholding taxes on construction contracts by local and foreign contractors?

117. What items of investment costs are subject to VAT? At what rate? What is the total amount of VAT? Is VAT amount already included in the figures presented? If VAT is refunded – what is the processing time and realistic delay in receiving the refunds?

118. Is the project charging VAT on its output? If yes, at what rate? Is VAT refundable? What inputs are subject to VAT? If VAT is levied, how quickly does the project receive a VAT refund, or is there a delay? How many months?

119. What operating items are subject to import duties, excise taxes or VAT? Have these taxes been properly included?

120. Is water and electricity exempted from sales tax or any other tax? Water and electricity prices are not subject to taxes as these are included in the tariff.

121. What personal income tax rates are applied to different labor categories employed by the project?

122. Are the project's local employees required to make social security contributions? If yes, what is the level required? Project is required to make such contributions on behalf of the local employees.

123. What is origin of banks - domestic or international? Would interest payments be subject to withholding tax?

124. What is origin of sub debt - domestic or international? Would interest payments be subject to withholding tax?

125. Withholding tax on dividends is set to 0%. Please confirm whether there is any withholding tax on dividends? on interest payments?

126. Who are the "various investors" in equity - domestic or international? Would dividends be subject to withholding tax?

127. The model has assumed a WHT of x%. However, this rate could be lower depending on the country where the loan provider is domiciled.

128. Withholding tax at x% is applicable on dividend distributed to shareholders. However, where shareholders are resident in countries that have a Double Tax Agreement (DTA). The DTA reduces the WHT rate from x% to y%.

VIII. INFLATION

129. Are the Capex figures adjusted for inflation? In other words, are they in nominal terms?

130. Are the cash items in the model in nominal or real terms? If nominal, why are they, cost items specifically, not changing over time to take into account the effect of inflation?

131. How/by whom is the PPA annual inflationary increase determined?

132. Why is inflation rate for tariffs higher than inflation for costs?

133. Please explain why the project uses different inflation rates for revenues and expenses, for instance; x% for capex items, y% for revenues, 4% for energy and other expenses and z% for land access? What is the rationale behind it?

134. From the financial model perspective, it looks like the chunk of the project costs is priced in USD; there would be a need to run a sensitivity test using US inflation rates to determine its impacts on project outcomes.

135. The discounting of net cash flows disregards the years of construction. All revenue items are over- valued because they are not discounted to year xxxx but are currently discounted to year yyyy. The cash flows for the calculation of NPV should be discounted x years back, to year xxxx not yyyy, assuming a construction period of x years.

IX. FOREX

136. Foreign exchange rate is fixed in nominal terms - this adds a diversion to cost projections.

137. At present, fixed nominal exchange rate in the model make future costs are understated. Repayment of foreign-denominated debt is also under-estimated. Model results are over-optimistic.

138. This is a project that derives all revenues in local currency. At the same time it's likely that some (or all) senior loans will be denominated in foreign currency. It's paramount to have a consistent projection and use of foreign exchange rates in the model. Fixed nominal exchange rates are not realistic. At present, fixed nominal exchange rate make future costs are understated. Repayment of foreign-denominated debt is also under-estimated.

139. Model is using USD as the model currency and all cash flow items are denominated in USD. If revenues are denominated in IRR and a portion of the loan is payable in IRR, we suggest a switch to IRR model. or alternatively, we recommend that all cash flow items to be reflected in their original currency and converted to model currency (here USD) using foreign exchange projection.

140. Can you please provide us with more information on how the Company is intending to hedge against the foreign exchange risk as well as against the fluctuation of oil prices?

X. RESIDUAL VALUE

141. What is the useful life of the project's assets for economic depreciation purposes? What is a realistic timeframe when the project assets can be used without major re-investment? The model does not include the residual values of the assets of the project.

142. Why is the terminal value greater than the initial value of assets by almost 2 times? The plant has been depreciating and there have not been any capital additions. The terminal value should be less than the initial value of plant assets.

XI. EQUITY

143. The Proposed deal is presented such that Bank finances 100% of initial capital costs (XXX million) and Sponsor does not spend anything (supplies only the technology and its business model). This does not fit the Bank's financing requirements.

144. The model assumes that Sponsors are using a pro-rata drawdown of equity and debt, while Lenders are demanding that 100% of equity is to be spent first.

145. The equity drawdown is negative (XXX million) in January 20xx. Is this is a refund or funds withdrawal from the project by the equity holders.

146. Core investor's equity: how much equity is available from sponsors? What is the proportion of equity that could be financed in cash? When is it available for the project? If the Capex overruns happen – who will be responsible for the payment?

147. Please confirm that all equity contribution (including contingent equity) is in cash, and not in the form of in-kind assets.

148. Does Government become a shareholder in the project by providing the land (worth USD XXX mln) or is this is a "grant"? If Government becomes a shareholder - what is its acquired share(s)? If this is a grant - how is the Government compensated for this? Government should become a shareholder and earn the dividend.

149. The project is highly leveraged with a Debt to Equity ratio of x:y.

150. There is very low level of equity contribution by the sponsor. The project will be funded by xx% equity, yy% debt and zz% revenues during construction.

151. What is the target return (i.e. cost) of equity to the equity holders? What is an "acceptable" equity return? (Nominal or real?)

152. Why was such a high rate of return on equity selected?

153. Unacceptable to Lenders: Interest on preference shares and dividends are paid immediately after completion, at the same time as senior debt.

154. What is "various investors" in equity - domestic or international? Would dividends be subject to withholding tax?

155. Equity investor exit has been modeled from 20xx, loan is repayable by 20xx. Shareholder exit prior to full debt repayment may not be acceptable to the lenders.

156. The calculation of XNPV (equity return) is based on dividend payment amounts only and does not take into account the equity draw downs. Please explain why this is so.

XII. SENIOR DEBT

157. The presentation on the debt is currently consolidated. It would be preferred if different tranches of debt can be indicated separately.

158. Who are the other DFIs and commercial banks potentially financing this transaction?

159. What is origin of banks other than Bank - domestic or international? Would interest payments be subject to withholding tax?

160. Loan tenor of xx years stated in the financial model. Does his correspond with the maximum limits by banks. If it is beyond the maximum limit, is there a logical justification for asking for xx years tenor?

161. What are the arguments behind step-up interest rate?

162. What are the arguments behind back-loading schedule of loan repayment?

163. The proposal is x year grace period with first installment commencing in 20xx. However operations commence in 20xx after a x year construction period and it is not clear why repayments cannot commence earlier as the project operates a full year in 20xx and has DSCR above the minimum threshold of x.

164. Grace on Interest Repayments is assumed to vary from x to y months on different tranches of debt, but banks cannot capitalize interest - interest accrued must be paid in cash.

165. I don't see upfront and appraisal fees calculation neither in Funding, nor in Debt. Are these fees included in the budget and cashflows?

166. Commitment and arrangement fee are on the low side. A minimum of x% for Arrangement fee and y% for commitment fee seems more in line with the pricing on similar facilities.

167. Margins of xxx bps are low. Since the the loan pricing is still under discussion, it has been the best practice in modeling that we use the higher end of margins, preferably at xxx bps or more. At this stage, this will allow us to have a comfort in the model results. Actual rates will be discussed in the due course.

168. LIBOR assumption of x% being fixed forever is not plausible, we need to put a realistic and conservative figure.

169. Commitment fee is treated as an up-front fee and as a result fees are underestimated. Base for the calculation of commitment fee is the undrawn amount of debt during drawdown periods.

170. Revise the formula for calculating semi-annual interest rate. Would it not be better to use the formula ((1+Annual interest rate)^(6/12)-1) to change annual interest rate to semiannual interest rate? - You are correct, though the difference is minor. Since that annual interest rate is small (1+r) ^(6/12)-1 ≈ 1+r*(6/12). However, if you are not satisfied with the approximation, we are happy to include the exact formula in the next versions of the model.

171. The calculation of Interest during construction is underestimated.

172. Bank X is not allowed to capitalize interest and fees, and all IDC(interest during construction) must be paid out in cash. Delete capitalized interest.

173. Is interest during construction capitalized or paid in cash? - The project draws down on the loan to pay the interest during construction and these calculations look at how much additional debt needs to be drawn to pay the interest. Here, the debt amount is circular or requires a macro to solve.

174. Why is only x% of interest during construction paid for every year, what happens to the remaining x%?

175. Why are mandatory prepayments subtracted from "loan balance end" and thus included as part of debt repayment? This reduces the opening debt repayment obligation due the following year.

176. This is a project that derives all revenues in local currency. At the same time it's likely that some (or all) senior loans will be denominated in foreign currency. It's paramount to have a consistent projection and use of foreign exchange rates in the model. Fixed nominal exchange rates are not realistic. At present, fixed nominal exchange rate make future costs are understated. Repayment of foreign-denominated debt is also under-estimated.

177. Principal repaid on Senior Debt Tranche A [Local] (XXXX million). Why is principal repaid during construction, which puts additional pressure on the capital structure? You should obtain longer grace on principal on principal Repaid on Senior Debt Tranche A.

178. The Inputs tab includes debt covenants. The indicative term sheet is required to make sure that the terms have been appropriately reflected in the model

XIII. BRIDGE LOAN / INTER-COMPANY LOAN

179. Confirm if there has been use of a loan bridging facility. Who has provided the loan and at what interest rate? What is the tenor and when is repayment expected?

180. Please kindly provide us with a capex plan as well as a pre-opex plan before completion. How has the bridge-loan been used?

181. Is there a bridge financing facility of XXX million for x months? What has been financed with the bridge financing facility? Is repayment of this facility included in project cash flows?

182. Re-financing of existing debt or bridge loan: Is there any potential lender that has agreed to refinance the debt?

183. Intercompany loan of USD XXX million. Logic and mechanism behind the intercompany loans? What are the companies involved?

What are the terms of the loan: tenor, interest rate, other fees, conditions of repayment of interest and principal, possibility of revolving credit, etc.?

XIV. MEZZ / SUB DEBT / JUNIOR DEBT / SHAREHOLDER LOANS

184. What is origin of sub debt - domestic or international? Would interest payments be subject to withholding tax?

185. Subordinated debt is presented by Sponsors as equity. This is only acceptable if sub debt is fully subordinated to senior debt, raising and ongoing fees and interest on sub debt are not paid in cash during construction, both interest and principal repayments of sub debt are only possible when dividend payout covenants are satisfied, and non-payment of fees/interest/principal of sub debt does not cause a default (nor a delayed default).

186. No penalty rate is being charged on the unpaid Shareholder loan interest. Please confirm that the shareholders agree with this approach.

187. In project memorandum, it is mentioned that subordinated interest and service fee will be charged on shareholder contribution. The model does not show anywhere that subordinated interest is paid.

188. Interest during construction on Shareholders Loan (at xx%) is not a cash cost to project investment costs, should not be included in uses of funds. Should not be included into cash item "Interest during construction for period".

189. Please indicate why payment of shareholder loan is not subject to covenants?

190. Unacceptable to Lenders: Interest on Investor's shares is paid immediately after completion, at the same time as senior debt. Almost the same amount of payout as senior principal debt. This early payout takes place before and during the period of the lowest DSCRs.

191. It would be preferable for the interest on shareholder loan to be accrued rather than cash-paid. This would allow interest to remain deductible for tax calculations but would render the conditions for dividend payout more convenient to draft and implement.

192. Interest and fees on mezzanine loan are not part of capex. Assumptions clearly say that mezzanine loan is part of equity and interest on mezzanine loan is not a project cost, it's a cost to equity holders. Consequently, this can not be treated as an asset that equity holders "contribute" to the project, because it's not an asset. Interest and fees on mezzanine loan must be removed from capital structure. These costs are to be borne by equity holders.

193. It's assumed that Interest on Mezzanine Funding and on Standby Mezzanine Funding is Paid During Construction. These two represent equity and such interest should not increase the total cost of the project. Interest should be capitalized and paid out later - subject to dividend lock-up rules.

194. Shareholder loans are supposed to be subordinated to senior debt and as such should not have a prior claim on the project revenues. It is proposed to reschedule repayment of shareholder loans to the period following the first loan repayment.

XV. DIVIDENDS

195. How much is the project expected to pay in dividends to the shareholders? What mechanism determines when and what dividends are to be paid?

196. Withholding tax on dividends is set to 0%. Confirm: Is there any withholding tax on dividends? on interest payments?

197. Dividend are paid even when no cash available. Dividend policy/ modeling needs to be clarified.

198. Is dividend distribution set as a minimum of "net cashflow available for distribution" (in Cashflow Statement) and "net income" (in Income Statement), or how the amount of distribution is determined?

199. For the last concession period, the dividends are being paid irrespective of the retained earnings balance which results in negative retained earnings balance. Please confirm this is as intended.

200. Dividend distribution starts in the same period as the senior debt repayment. This is too early and should be rescheduled. The dividend payment should be subject to the current conditions in the model plus meeting a target DSCR achieved in a period, comparable with the dividend lockup ratio of x or higher, plus other dividend lockup rules to be specified in the course of the appraisal.

201. Distribution of dividends starts immediately after construction, while first repayment of loan principal is requested to be postponed until 12 months after construction. Given the strength of projected cashflows, such a grace period can be somewhat shortened?

XVI. CASH WATERFALL

202. Model does not have a proper cash waterfall and it's very confusing to figure out seniority and subordination of various cash flow items. Make sure that the cash waterfall in our model gets documented in loan documentation, with clear sequence of all cash items in order of seniority.

203. Sponsors offered x% cash-sweep to senior debt providers, and it should be placed in cash water fall after senior debt, after DSRA, but before Cash balance account, and before sub debt.

204. Management Incentive Fee of USD XXXXX per year should be subordinated to senior debt, and be performance-based, i.e. if the project is not doing so well - the fee can't be paid out in full.

205. Two expense items should be subordinated to senior debt, and be performance-based, i.e. if the project is not doing so well - the fee can't be paid out in full: Sponsor Charges of USD XXX per year and Management Incentive Fee of USD XXXX per year.

206. Payment of Shareholder Loan Principal and Sale of assets - should be subordinated to DSRA and to Maintenance Reserve Acc. DSRA should come first, Maintenance Reserve Acc second, and then - Payment of Shareholder Loan Principal and Sale of assets.

207. Please indicate why free cash flow (net cash flow after dividends) in year 20xx and 20xx are negative?

XVII. RESERVE ACCOUNTS (DEBT SERVICE RESERVE AC-COUNT « DSRA », MAJOR MAINTENANCE RESERVE ACCOUNT "MMRA", A DEBT SERVICE ACCRUAL ACCOUNT "DSAA", ETC.)

208. Funding of DSRA is zero in the uses of Funds statement?

209. How is the DSRA pre-funding amount determined? - The DSRA balance is required to be at least equal to the succeeding 6 months' senior debt service (principal + interest). Around the time of financial close, this was fixed for contractual purposes at EUR XXX m.

210. the cash flow impact of DSRA (release and financing of DSRA during operation) in not included in the cash flow statement.

211. No provision for the Maintenance Reserve Account is currently made. Confirm how maintenance requirements will be catered for?

212. Debt Service Payment Account: Could you please explain what the use of the Debt Service Payment Account (DSPA) is? Does it correspond to a Debt Service reserve account?

213. How has the MMRA prefunding amount been determined? - The MMRA required balance depends on forecast major maintenance expenditures over the succeeding x years.

XVIII. DEBT RATIOS

214. Unacceptable to Lenders: Debt service ratios are low in 20xx-20xx. We look for DSCR ratios (without DSRA) of 1.x. Given the fact that the model contains (i) very early payout of dividends; and (ii) early payout of interest on IDC shares – there is sufficient room to improve the ratios by postponing dividend and shares interest payout to periods when DSCR is above 1.x.

215. As described in the terms sheet, the Debt Service Coverage Ratio (DSCR) is obtained by dividing the aggregate: (1) EBITDA for such calculation period - Taxes paid - All capital expenditures; by the aggregate of: (2) All scheduled repayments that fell during such calculation period. Why is this definition different from the conventional definition of DSCR obtained by dividing the aggregate: (A) Revenues for such calculation period - Taxes paid - Opex - Capex +/- Change in working capital; by the aggregate: (B) Interest and principal debt repayments for such calculation period? The resulting sets of ratios under the two methods are different.

216. The definition of DSCRs as described in the terms sheet excludes the change in working capital, while it is a significant use of cash in running the business operations. Below, we compute and compare a set of DSCRs according to the definition of the terms sheet and the conventional definition.

217. The calculation of senior debt and senior DSCR should not include the subordinated debt which is compensated for this subordination through preferential interest rates.

218. Loan disbursements by the shareholders should not be part of the enumerator in the calculation of DSCR

219. Why Commercial Bank Agency Fee is excluded from calculation of debt ratios? If I understand correct, this is a cash item paid by the project, and it's included in total interest in cashflow. Such exclusion overstates the debt service ratios.

220. The DSCRs computed by the Sponsor are "annualized" and the DSCRs computed by Bank are reported on a semi-annual basis.

221. How will the debt service during construction be repaid if the revenues during construction are not realized as planned?

XIX. SENSITIVITY / SCENARIOS

222. Model does not include sensitivity analysis

223. Only the high case scenario has been considered. It would be more interesting to have projections in the low case scenario.

224. Traffic scenarios are not shown to us. We would like to see all traffic scenarios.

225. Volume projection used in base case is the highest among the 5 projections available. Why this projection is taken as the base case?

226. An explanation should be provided in the financial model assumption book regarding the differences between a low case and high case pricing scenarios.

227. What are the underlying assumptions on the low case price scenario and how is this scenario different from the base case price scenario?

228. Under what circumstances will the scenarios change and what is the probability of the other two scenarios from the base case happening?

229. One of the main functions of the financial model should be to enable sensitivity test on the key assumptions. Currently sensitivity parameters are not included in the model and due to the structure of the model, it is not possible to incorporate sensitivity without structural changes on the model mechanics and structure.

230. There is no sensitivity test (cost overrun) on capex under EPC contract. How are the EPC cost increase due to changes in the project scope and some other unforeseen events covered? - The EPC Contract is a Lump Sum Turn Key contract which is by definition a fixed cost contract. Applying a sensitivity is not relevant for this item (though the label of the cell may be misleading, I agree). The unforeseen events are borne by the contractor as per the terms of the EPC Contract. Changes of project scope are pre-agreed in any case between the Sponsor and the Contractor through amendments of the EPC Contract. Any changes outside of the scope of the EPC contract are covered off by the additional equity amount, whose value is still under negotiation.

231. Capex do not change with delays. Is it realistic to assume so bearing in mind that Capex, taxes and IDCs are subject to fluctuations?

232. From the financial model perspective, it looks like the chunk of the project costs is priced in USD; there would be a need to run a sensitivity test on US inflation rate to see its impacts on project outcomes.

233. The NPV and IRR values for the base case presented in sheet "Sensitivity" do not match with the ones calculated in sheet "NPV & IRR"? They may be leftovers of former version but in this case should be deleted.

234. What is the basis for the different Price Scenarios 1, 2 & 3?

235. Need for more clarification on how sensitivities on shutdowns and OPEX are run.

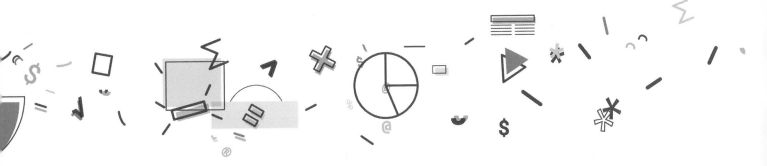

AUTOR **HEDIEH KIANYFARD**
DESIGN **MILTON BORDEIRA**

FiNEXMOD